Penguin Handbooks
The Wines of Burgundy

H. W. Yoxall was born in 1896 and educated at St Paul's
School and Balliol College, Oxford, where he was a
classical scholar. He served in the First World War,
winning the Military Cross and Bar. At the end of 1917
he was seconded to the British Military Mission in the
United States. He has been Director, then Managing
Director, then Chairman of the Anglo-American firm
Condé-Nast Publications, President of the Periodical
Proprietors' Association and Vice-President of the
International Federation of the Periodical Press. He has
been a Justice of the Peace for many years and has twice
been Chairman of the Bench. He is a Governor of the
Star and Garter Home for Disabled Ex-Servicemen and
was awarded the O.B.E. for his magisterial and charitable
services. In 1972 he was elected Chairman of the
International Wine and Food Society. He is a
Commander of the Confrérie du Tastevin and a
Chevalier de l'Ordre Bretvin. His previous books include
*Modern Love, All Abroad, Journey into Faith, A Fashion of
Life* and *The Enjoyment of Wine*.

H. W. Yoxall

The Wines
of Burgundy

Penguin Books

Penguin Books Ltd, Harmondsworth,
Middlesex, England
Penguin Books Australia Ltd, Ringwood,
Victoria, Australia

First published by The International Wine & Food Society 1968
Published in Penguin Books 1974

Copyright © Harry W. Yoxall, 1968

Made and printed in Great Britain by
Richard Clay (The Chaucer Press), Ltd,
Bungay, Suffolk
Set in Monotype Bembo

Contents

6 Contents

Preface

The publisher of the Wine & Food Society's books, in whose series this volume first appeared, sets out their scope as being 'aimed at the intelligent middle market, the members of which already know something of the subject and are interested in knowing more'.

A prudent author follows the instructions of his publisher, and this book is therefore intended to fall within these terms of reference. It will, on the one hand, presume at least an elementary knowledge of vine-growing and wine-making, and will not dilate on these subjects except where burgundy presents any special peculiarities. On the other hand it will certainly not be an advanced treatise intended, for example, for aspirants to the Master of Wine examination. I could, of course, pad its pages with scientific detail (acquired at second hand) about Kimmeridgian beds, malic acids, Oechsle standards and other technicalities. But that is not my intention.

I want simply to write about a wine I love, and hope that my views – not expert, but certainly experienced – may bring a greater enjoyment of it to the reader. I believe that an exchange of knowledge and opinion is the best means of heightening the appreciation of wine, burgundy or any other. The opinions expressed in these pages will, rightly or wrongly, be personal. It is not a text-book, but perhaps it might be called a test book – the outcome of tests over years of pleasant trial and enlightening error.

The history of Burgundy will be compressed, in these pages, into aspects of vinous interest. However I must, for reference, set out the geography of the area in some detail, and list its better-known products, ordinary as well as superior, as a guide both for tourism and buying. The quality of a wine is best indicated, in the first instance, by the locality of its vineyard.

But second only to this in importance – if indeed it is secondary – is the type of grape used. I have seen it stated by one writer that it is unnecessary for the amateur wineman to clutter his mind with varietal types as well as with place names. I take leave to differ from this 'authority'. So without going deeply into viticultural botany I shall distinguish between the *pinots*, the *chardonnays*, the *gamays* and the *aligotés* which do so much to establish the character of the various growths of burgundy.

I feel that the time is ripe for such a publication, if only because burgundy – or at any rate its finer *crus* – has been overwhelmed in the popular mind by the sheer volume of bordeaux. But there are other reasons too. In the first place burgundy, in my opinion, is very much misunderstood in Anglo-Saxon countries, where it is regarded as a heavy wine. It is a full wine, but not heavy. I shall therefore have to refer frequently to the bases of this misconception.

There is also a feeling that claret is more homogeneous, and therefore more reliable, than burgundy. This is partially true, but it makes the discovery of good burgundy, in all price ranges, the more gratifying, indeed exciting. A proper understanding of these points (by which of course I mean my understanding) may serve to increase the enjoyment of a wine that ranges from the noblest growths, the peers of any region's, to a variety of sound table wines still relatively inexpensive even in these days of inordinate inflation.

Then there has been the recent controversy about the 'faking' of burgundy. This appears to be proceeding towards a happy issue, but it seems necessary to include in the book some of the old cautions until we are completely assured that malpractices have been eliminated. But while Burgundy has perhaps been more plagued by false labels than other wine areas, it is by no means the only one to suffer from such traps for the unwary.

I should explain certain decisions about the nomenclature used in the following chapters. *Cépage*, for breed, growth or species of grape, seems an unnecessary Gallicism, and will generally be anglicized. *Finage* is the Burgundian word for what is called a *commune* elsewhere. In fact it is, to all intents and purposes, a *commune*, and to repeat this unusual local term of *finage*, when it will be cropping up frequently, would seem to me pedantic. One might turn it into 'parish', on the principle of anglicizing wherever possible; but 'parish' perhaps sounds excessively English in a wine book, besides suggesting an ecclesiastical subdivision rather than a civil one. So for *finage* I shall use *commune*, and print it without a capital (see the next paragraph but four).

Another term with which writers like to parade their special knowledge is the Burgundian *climat* for 'vineyard'. I shall just use 'vineyard', indicating a plot of vines, whether under single or multiple ownership, in a physically defined area. *Vigneron*, literally a vineyard worker, generally, in Burgundy, means its proprietor; if so, let him be 'proprietor' or 'grower' – for let it be remembered that in ninety-nine cases out of a hundred in Burgundy he makes the wine from the grapes that he grows. *Négociant*, the blender and wholesaler, who is often incidentally a proprietor too, can, I think, be rendered as 'shipper'.

Then there is the question of *Appellation d'Origine Contrôlée*, the name to which a wine is entitled under the intricate but beneficent and fairly effective regulations governing burgundy. I propose to refer to this as 'the *appellation*', with the italics indicating that it is the technical French word, and to use *AC* as the adjectival form.

I must warn readers that several Burgundian vineyards are known by two different names, and that in many cases the spelling of the names has one or more variants. When the vineyard would not be readily recognizable in the version I have adopted, I have mentioned the alternative name also.

For the sake of brevity I shall use the shortest intelligible rendering for place- or wine-names. Thus Le Clos de Vougeot will be described as Clos Vougeot. I shall leave out the definite article whenever possible, e.g. Chablis Grenouilles for Chablis les Grenouilles. But occasionally a *le* or *les* is essential to mark a special *climat* – sorry, vineyard; for example Le Montrachet, Les St-Georges. Saint, as shown by the preceding sentence, I shall always render as St; but when vineyard names look odd without their *de*, *du* or *des*, these will be included. Ch. is an obvious abbreviation for Château, though there are not many of these in the Burgundy vineyards.

This leads to problems of typography. Generally, I think, capital letters should be avoided whenever possible. I have done this above with regard to grape names. We do not commonly employ capital initials for a flower – rose, for example. Why then for a grape? So let *pinot* be *pinot*, not *Pinot*. Similarly with generic wines. When I refer to the wine, burgundy, I shall use a small b; Burgundy refers to the area. So chablis from Chablis, beaujolais from the Beaujolais, and so on. But when it comes to reference to particular vineyards the lower-case initial, as printers call it, seems to look peculiar. One can hardly write of a gevrey-chambertin, still less of a beaune clos des mouches, without an appearance of oddity. Accordingly I shall not aim at pedantic consistency, but write my names as seems most natural and intelligible.

Having suffered from many lazy wine books that express output indifferently in *tonneaux*, hectolitres, gallons, etc. I have tried to convert all my figures into the readily intelligible numbers of bottles, or – when these would run into too many digits – of cases; cases, of course, of twelve standard burgundy bottles of 75 centilitres each. A gallon, incidentally, is just over six bottles. And though we are all going to be metricated soon, I have decided, in regard to land measurements, to speak in terms of the acres we know rather than of the hectares about which we shall have to learn. A traditional Burgundian land measurement that appears in certain learned books is the *ouvrée*. This represents about a tenth of an acre.

There is another preliminary that must be mentioned – my acknowledgement of profound gratitude for advice received from Mr Ronald Avery (Avery & Co. Ltd, Bristol), Etienne Barbot (Beaune), Georges Bouchard (Bouchard Ainé, Beaune), Jacques Chevignard (Grand Chambellan de la Confrérie des Chevaliers du Tastevin, Nuits-St-Georges), Yves Colombot, Robert Drouhin (Joseph Drouhin & Cie, Beaune), René Engel (Vosne-Romanée), Pierre Forgeot (Secretary-General of the Comité Professionel du Bourgogne, Beaune), Julian Jeffs, Louis Latour (Louis Latour & Cie, Beaune), Philippe Marion (Chanson Père & Fils, Beaune), le Comte de Moucheron (de Moucheron & Cie, Meursault), André Noblet (Chef de Cave, Domaine de la Romanée-Conti), Philippe Poupon (Calvet & Cie, Beaune), the late Guy Prince, Harvey Prince (J. L. P. Lebègue & Co. Ltd, London), Michel Rémon (A. Regnard & Fils, Chablis), Peter Reynier, MC (J. B. Reynier Ltd, London), the late André Simon, C.B.E., Jean Thorin jr (J. Thorin & Cie, Pontanevaux) and Aubert de Vilaine (Domaine de la Romanée-Conti). None of these gentlemen, however, is to be held responsible for the opinions that I shall enunciate, though each has helped to shape some of them to a greater or lesser extent.

As to the many books that I have read, I shall append a bibliography of those I have found most useful, in part or in whole, with regard to my subject. All of them, I am sure, display greater expertise than I possess; but certain of these writings are by their nature too summary for a full coverage of burgundy, while others are too long or too technical for the common reader.

So perhaps such an intermediate production as this may find an unassuming but acceptable place on the shelves of the wine-lover's library. These shelves, by the way, are the second most important part of his equipment, coming only after the contents of his cellar.

This book was originally written in 1967, but has been brought up to date, in all matters that change, to the spring of 1973.

Finally, I have never yet read any wine books in which I have not spotted some inconsistencies and indeed errors. It is too much to hope that such will not have crept into this one. For these I apologize in advance, and hope that they will prove to be unimportant.

1. The Wine of Burgundy

The Slopes of Gold – is there any regional name anywhere in the world at once so poetically evocative and so practically descriptive? Is there any other ribbon of agricultural land with so rich an output per acre? Indeed, I should hazard a guess that no mining area of equivalent size has so high a capital value. For mines represent wasting assets, while burgundy, made for over fifteen hundred years, can go on being made indefinitely.

I have turned the name of the Côte d'Or into the plural, not just because this is more euphonious in English, but because *côte* represents a small range rather than a single hill.

It has taken a series of long chances to produce the miraculous combination accounting for the burgundy of the Slopes of Gold. First there is the right kind of soil: the limestone edge, rich in minerals, of the alluvial valley of the Saône, once (like most rivers) much wider than it is now. Next, the perfect elevation and orientation of the slight hills that formerly contained the river on its westward limits; hills not too precipitous nor too shallow, with folds facing mostly south-east at the perfect angle to catch the most beneficial morning sun. Then came the breeding of noble species of grapes, to extract the finest value from soil and climate. Finally a long history of patient experiment and devoted craftsmanship, providing the human capital needed for the full exploitation of these gifts of nature.

But each of these jewels of fortune has its reverse side. The soil is not only thin in content, as it should be for *vitis vinifera*, which, like man, thrives on struggle. It is also narrow in extent. The finest Slopes of Gold are little more than a quarter of a mile wide; only at the southern end does the width exceed a mile, and that barely. The average width is 700 yards. Further, from north to south the whole length is little over twenty-five miles. So the total output is exiguous in comparison with that of the other great wine areas.

Meanwhile within this area perfection is even more strictly confined. A few yards too far up the slopes the vines became too exposed to absorb complete nourishment, and do not ripen fully. A few yards too near the eastern edge the soil becomes over-rich and the elevation insufficient; hence easy wine, flat and unremarkable. (To preserve an even quality in the wine the slopes must be picked horizontally, and not from summit to base.)

Then these slopes that turn themselves precisely to welcome the warmth and nourishment of the sunlight are situated precariously far north in latitude for a wine-land. It is the furthest north, in fact, of all the famous areas except Champagne and the German fields. Therefore spring comes late; there is always danger of insufficient sun, frequently damage by frosts and later by hailstorms, to diminish the normally modest quantity and increase the cost of the harvest that survives these hazards. (In 1967, for example, many fields suffered serious frost in May, and many that had escaped this experienced devastating hail in August.) The use of vintage cards has been overdone in general, but with reference to burgundy it is important to memorize the more equable, sunnier years that yield naturally good wines. Alternatively the amateur must find a conscientious merchant who has watched the weather and will provide his own knowledge to guide his selections.

So the enjoyment of fine burgundy is always a somewhat expensive privilege, and for some good but specially difficult years it is costly indeed. Alec Waugh, in his *In Praise of Wine*, quotes one of George Meredith's characters as pitying another because he had an income of only £600 a year and a passion for burgundy. And one knows what £600 represented a hundred years ago. But somehow, in the last third of the twentieth century, one still manages to afford to buy burgundy.

Then the excellence of the noble grapes of Burgundy involves a corresponding niggardliness of output, and a temptation to vineyard-owners to use more exuberant species – 'the lesser breeds without the Law' – with consequent increase of quantity but decrease of quality. In the last thirty years the strict rulings of the *appellation* have controlled the employment of inferior grapes. If used, they must be declared on the label. But these regulations apply to France only. For wines exported, other than in bottles, the onus for the obedience to these regulations is still thrown on the honour and traditions of the importer. Of the conscientious kind there is, fortunately, a plenty; but there is also, alas, much equivocation to trap the unwary buyer.

Even history, which for long favoured the development of burgundy, took a nasty turn a hundred and eighty years ago. From almost the beginning of recorded viticulture the best Burgundy vineyards fell progressively into the ownership of the monasteries. These alone, during centuries of continuous banditry and intermittent warfare, could afford the constant care and patient workmanship that owners involved in secular struggles could not provide. Only in the quiet of the cloister could wines be kept from year to year and brought, not indeed to the perfection that we have known recently, but to something better than the quality of *vin de consommation courante* that lay production achieved, with each year's output thirstily consumed from the wood within a few months of the vintage.

But at the time of the French Revolution these ecclesiastical properties, where the art of wine-making had been carried to the highest pitch of those times, were all dispossessed. The church vineyards, thrown onto the market at a time of economic stress, were savagely divided into small lots to suit current purchasing power. Then the original speculators sub-divided them again for the peasants, into thousands of patches too small for the finesse of cultivation that such northern fields demand. The process was later extended by French laws of inheritance, to cause a further fragmentation of parcels already too diminutive. Only recently, and only on a very small scale, has the process of reconsolidation set in. But improvement in vinting has also been effected by the activities of shippers who blend the wines of the smallest proprietors, and so bring a high average level of skill to the making of burgundy.

I shall say more about this 'democracy' of ownership in Burgundy in Chapter 2, and more about the burgundy grapes in Chapter 3; but the most important thing is the wine itself. What kind of a wine is burgundy?

So far I have been writing only about the Côte d'Or, the source of the great wines. Naturally I shall discuss, later, the other fields entitled to the burgundy *appellation*. Some people regret that this was not confined to the Côte d'Or, and perhaps to its isolated outpost at Chablis. They feel that the Chalonnais, the Mâconnais, the Beaujolais – not to mention the *ordinaire* fields of outer Burgundy – should be grouped under another title. This would certainly have simplified matters for wine-scribes and – what is more important – avoided confusion among wine-drinkers.

However that may be, it has not been done. A bottle of Romanée-Conti and of Mâcon *rouge*, of Le Montrachet and of beaujolais *aligoté*, is each equally entitled to be called burgundy. It has to be remembered, however, that similar difficulties must be faced in writing of bordeaux. The Bordelais also includes vast areas of *ordinaire* fields outside the aristocratic vineyards of the Haut Médoc, Graves, Sauternes, Barsac, St Emilion and Pomerol.

Even on the Côte d'Or the merely good is geographically intertwined with the very good. You can step a hundred yards or so from the Domaine de la Romanée-Conti and find just decent *commune* wines, of no particular *cuvée*, being legitimately made under the name of Vosne-Romanée.

So we must take the title of 'burgundy', even as applied only to the Côte d'Or, as being all-embracing for quality, from wine as fine as is made anywhere to wine of a merit that could be achieved in many other fields. In passing, though, we should note that no other area in the world attains such a high level of both red and white table wines.

But whatever the quality, there is still a certain similarity of kind covering the whole range. I come back, after some digressions, to my previous question: what kind of a wine is burgundy?

There is a common feeling, most prevalent in the United Kingdom, that red burgundy is a heavy wine. A widespread notion places it, for weight, halfway between claret and port. Perhaps it is because of their acceptance of this misconception that many British merchants demand of their shippers a heavy-ish *cuvée*, said to be suitable for our northern climate.

How does this heaviness come about? First, knowing that the wine is intended for the British market, the shipper will select what he believes to be wanted from the thousands of samples offered by the proprietors; for these thousands each have a different style. To get these heavy weights prolonged fermentation will have been required, whereas the trend of burgundy vinification for the French market is towards a quicker fermentation – of which I shall say more in Chapter 14.

Wines that are the product of a slow fermentation are normally kept longer in the cask before bottling, whereas the wines of the quicker fermentation should be bottled earlier, to give a fresher, less ponderous substance. This early bottling does produce a delicious liveliness, though at the cost of reducing the wine's duration.

Some critics of the heavy style of red burgundy attribute it to excessive chaptalization. Chaptalization is, in plain English, the addition of sugar. Chaptal, one of Napoleon's greatest ministers, who wished to promote the consumption of the native beet-sugar, advocated its addition to the grape-juice, and the process became legally endorsed.

Now sugar is a natural ingredient of wine, and chaptalization is not objectionable *per se*. It has the effect of increasing the alcoholic strength of the wine, and in a northern area like Burgundy this is necessary in poor vintages. Unhappily it has become the practice every year, even when it is unnecessary, for a great deal of red burgundy.

Further, it is done not only too often, but too much. To increase the alcoholic strength of wine by 1°, which should surely be enough, 3¾ lb. of sugar is all that is needed in 22 gallons. (I translate approximately from the French measures.) This, in fact, already represents over four tenths of an ounce of added sugar per bottle. But chaptalization is permitted up to 6·58 lb. in 22 gallons, which is eight tenths of an ounce of added sugar per bottle. Naturally this sugar increases the volume of the wine, and so the vintner's revenue, and there is always therefore a temptation to indulge in it to the full.

The process can only be executed, at the time of the fermentation, in the presence of an Excise representative (for picturesque detail I may add that he requires three days' notice in writing, which represents a pretty quick response for a government official). So probably the limit is never exceeded. But certainly the limit seems too high, and only in an abysmal year should it be reached for wine of quality.

Two things may be noted here in passing: first, chaptalization is never used for good white burgundies, which are intrinsically stronger than the reds; and it is undesirable even for the poor whites, as it creates difficulties in their making. Secondly, it is not confined to Burgundy. It is permitted in Bordeaux, and is increasingly being accepted for common clarets, despite all the principles of the Bordeaux purists.

So then, if excessive chaptalization is not the general cause, what explains the loaded taste of much of the red burgundy sold in the United Kingdom, and of some sold in the United

States? Can it be an admixture of heavier wine from the Rhône – or even from the Midi? (This will be considered in greater detail in Chapter 15.) Can it even be the addition of a touch of brandy? Perish the thought, you will say – though brandy is added to port and sherry. Whatever the explanation, I recommend the beginner to ask his merchant for the kind of red burgundy they drink in Burgundy, which is not a heavy wine at all.

Here one comes up against the difficulties of descriptive epithets for wine. Some of those used are admittedly far-fetched, and embarrassing to the ordinary amateur. But I think everyone with some experience can distinguish between a *heavy* wine, which burgundy should not be, and a *full* wine, which burgundy is, white as well as red.

It is always a full wine, with plenty of flavour. The Côte de Beaune, the southern half of the Côte d'Or, produces softer red wines, it is true, than the more northerly Côte de Nuits, but they are all rich in taste, rich in authority. At the Poste at Beaune I recently drank a Beaune Bressandes '57 (itself a big year) which was a very full wine – particularly for this Côte – such as we are supposed to favour in England. It is fine when you get a naturally big wine, but there are too many artificially big burgundies to be found in the British market.

Burgundy, writes André Simon in *The Noble Grapes and the Great Wines of France*, is, compared with claret, 'more robust, more assertive, more immediately obvious'. But behind the immediate impact there lie, in the better *cuvées*, infinite subtleties. Hoffmann, by the way – he of the *Contes* – said that a musical composer who wanted to write heroic music should drink burgundy.

Try any red burgundy, sip for sip, against any red bordeaux of similar quality and maturity (which will usually call for the bordeaux to be older than the burgundy), and I think you will at once perceive the more emphatic flavour of the burgundy. For that reason, it goes better with the more fully-flavoured meats such as mutton, and with game. Similarly the bouquet of the burgundy is likely to be more pronounced, though sometimes more evanescent.

Some authorities speak of burgundy as the 'masculine wine'. Perhaps 'more masculine' is acceptable, so long as this does not imply that the femininity of bordeaux is weakness, but rather suppleness and grace.

Comparing any selected samples of the two wines in this manner, no reasonably experienced drinker would have much difficulty in differentiating between them. But when it comes to a single red wine served anonymously in a decanter, the beginner may take comfort from the fact that it is often very hard even for the professional to be certain whether it is burgundy or bordeaux, particularly if the bordeaux is a St-Emilion or even a St-Estèphe, the fullest of the Médocs. I have seen shippers of repute, and even growers, uncertain about a single red wine, tasted blind.

It has often been pointed out that the best way for the beginner to tell burgundy from bordeaux is to take a glance at the shape of the bottle. And here I shall fire a personal round in the eternal, unnecessary controversy concerning the comparative merits of these two great red wines. The harmoniously graduated curves of the burgundy bottle are to me aesthetically more pleasing than the bordeaux shape. The natural shoulders recall old mezzotints of gracious Victorian beauties, while claret bottles remind me of those square, padded effects that were made fashionable by couturiers in the unfortunate mode that prevailed before the Second World War.

The burgundy shape, too, is historically more authentic. It is closer to the original contour of the wine bottle as it first developed from the *pichet*, when better methods of vinting and the improvement of the cork stopper began to make it possible to store wine on its side, for long periods, in the bin. By such storage we learned the highest possibilities of wine – which we have known, by the way, for hardly two hundred years.

It may be noted in passing that all bottles used in Burgundy, whether for red wine or white, are dark green. I deplore the practice of some British shippers who use white glass for white burgundy, though this is proper for white bordeaux.

But if he cannot see the bottle, here is another hint for the beginner, to facilitate his attempts to distinguish between burgundy and claret. Again matching equal quality and maturity, claret always seems to be drier, slightly more austere.

I reject the common allegation that burgundy is a sweet wine. Indeed, the northern situation necessarily deprives its natural state of excess sugar; and sugar added, in proper quantities, in chaptalization should be converted into alcohol. But burgundy is generally fruitier than claret, more redolent of the grape. At least until it begins to fade with age it is, for better or worse, less ascetic in taste than claret.

I had just written the first draft of the preceding paragraph when I was invited to lunch by a hospitable London shipper who is one of the leaders of the trade. With one course we tasted two bottles of Clos Vougeot '59, the wine of both from the same well-known shipper on the Côte d'Or, but one of them bottled in Burgundy and one of them in London by my host. Candour compels me to admit that one of these was suave, almost sugary. And the surprising thing was that the sweeter drink was that bottled in France. Perhaps it may be said that the Frenchman knew he was making the wine for the British market.

A little later I shared a bottle of Echézeaux '49, French-bottled by an excellent shipper, which too was distinctly sweet. It almost had the quality of a fine old tawny port! Perhaps in each case the result was due to unnecessary chaptalization. I am not enough of a technician to be certain, but it may be that '49 and '59, big years both, did not need sugar at all, and its addition produced this excessive sweetness.

For characteristic red burgundy retains a good deal of acid in its flavour. Nevertheless it is not as dry as claret, and it gets less dry as you go south in Burgundy. To adapt an old phrase, the nearer the Beaune the sweeter the wine. But in fact many drinkers, particularly in countries that favour port, like a little suavity in their red table wine also, and find red bordeaux a little too austere.

The climate of Burgundy sometimes forces the cellar-masters, in very cold years, to warm the rooms in which the fermenting vats stand, to produce the necessary vigour in the fermentation. Some Bordelais critics fasten on this fact to describe burgundy as a 'cooked' wine, as if it were made like madeira. This is an absurd exaggeration. To meet the difficulties arising out of crude methods of heating, temperature-control is being increasingly introduced into the cellars of the better-equipped shippers; and this is one modern invention that should certainly improve wine – I am dubious of certain others.

To conclude the perennial but futile comparison of the two greatest red wines, even the stoutest Burgundian must concede that there is much more good claret about than good burgundy. But I think he might claim that the rarest perfection of burgundy is more exquisite than that of claret – if only because it is more rare. Perhaps too, at the middle of the scale, he might assert that a well-made *AC commune* wine of the Côte d'Or is as good as some of the lesser classified *crus* of the Médoc, and better than most *crus bourgeois*. Finally, Bordeaux has no red wine as good, at its price, for daily drinking as genuine beaujolais.

But wine, besides its bouquet and taste, also has something that we call texture. 'Velvety' is the epithet most often applied to the texture of burgundy; but if I am right about the burgundy drunk in France, it is really a chiffon velvet. Personally I experience the passage of burgundy over the tongue and down the throat as silken; though with certain anonymous bottlings I must confess that I have been reminded rather of raw silk.

There can be no dispute that Burgundy produces better white

table wine than Bordeaux. Indeed it is surely beyond argument that Burgundy produces the finest white table wines of the world. None other has its body, none other its fine natural grapey bouquet. But less than a quarter of the output of burgundy is white.

There are a few good dry white bordeaux, but their dryness always seems to me to betray a certain artificial quality, to have been achieved by an effort. The really fine white bordeaux are dessert wines, the sauternes and barsacs.

So too with the comparison of white burgundy and German wines. The latter are at their finest in the *Beerenauslese* and *Trockenbeerenauslese* ranges, which again are dessert wines. The less sweet Germans are more fragile, more precarious than the white burgundies for drinking with food. Their celebrated bouquets sometimes seem to me to be a little overforced, to relate more to perfumery than to vinting. To introduce again the vulgar factor of price, good white burgundies are cheaper than German wines of comparable merit.

White burgundies have been far less doctored than reds. Full, firm and authoritative, with an admirable balance of sugars and acids, they are incomparable drinks for accompanying all kinds of fish, *charcuterie* and cold meats. And the superior growths challenge the best red wines, from their own area or others, even with hot white meats and poultry.

2. The Burgundy Wine Trade

All the various compilations of statistics of Burgundy wine areas and ownership seem to differ from each other, as statistics have a way of doing; but all agree in giving a common picture of thousands of proprietors of small, indeed tiny, vineyards. There are very few substantial estates.

Now peasant-ownership of this kind is not uncommon in the winelands of the world, but in no other great table-wine area are the vineyards so fragmented.

Opposite are the relevant figures given by the Comité Professionel du Bourgogne, which should be authoritative, for the four *départements* that produce burgundy. They were those given when this book was first published and there has been some expansion since, but not enough to alter the general picture.

The *AC* wines are those bottled in France under the present 114 *appellations* authorized for burgundy, from the proudest Romanée-Conti or Montrachet to *bourgogne grand ordinaire* or petit chablis, or exported for bottling overseas with the *AC* guarantee. The non-*AC* are used for cheaper blended wines or as the *vins de consommation courante* that you can get in a French bar. But also (I fear) a good deal of this has come to Great Britain to be blended here with *AC* burgundies, and indeed with other wines, and sold by the less scrupulous under Burgundian titles, even under *commune* names.

Now, as will be seen later in this book, an appreciable number of the holdings are much larger than the average; therefore, if my mathematics are correct, an appreciable number must be smaller than the average. So you have thousands of proprietors cultivating an acre of vines or less. And in the Yonne area, once very extensive but greatly reduced since the phylloxera plague of the late nineteenth century, of the 2,470 acres of *AC* vineyards divided between some 8,000 owners, only some 1,200 are Chablis proper, so you may well wonder where much of the so-called chablis comes from. These figures explain much of the unevenness of burgundy, even when it is fully genuine.

| | Acreage | | No. of | Average acres per |
	AC	Non-AC	proprietors	proprietor
Côte d'Or	12,350	9,633	16,850	1·30
Saône-et-Loire (Chalonnais and Mâconnais)	14,820	22,724	42,710	0·88
Rhône (Beaujolais)	34,827	15,067	23,100	2·16
Yonne (inc. Chablis)	2,470	7,904	14,670	0·70
Total Burgundy	64,467	55,328	97,330	1·23

Now for the figures of output. I do not want to burden the reader with statistics, but instead of just taking an average I think it might be interesting to show the last five vintages for which I have figures, so that it may be seen how the output varies from year to year, and within districts (owing to local weather). As I have said, for intelligibility I have decided to translate all enumerations of output from the metric measures into bottles or cases of a dozen bottles. On page 27 is the picture of 1971 back to 1967, in round numbers, with the *AC* wines first, which are all that really ought to concern us. I may say that I got the figures from four different 'official' sources, and that none of them agreed; but the discrepancies were not great, and in any event I have rounded them off to the nearest 500 cases.

But of course the statistics give an exaggerated idea of the quantity available for bottling and casing. Not all of the wine can be retained for drinking; some 10% is lost by evaporation, etc. And much of what remains is never bottled, but consumed from the wood for the carafe trade (particularly with beaujolais), even from the minor *AC appellations*. If at first glance this output might still seem adequate, one must remember that it has to satisfy the thirst of the whole world – and a higher proportion of burgundy is exported than of any other French wine. The figures are very small indeed by comparison with those of Bordeaux, which has an output several times bigger than that of Burgundy. All the vineyards of Burgundy, as has been seen, cover only 120,000 acres; those of the Gironde cover some 350,000. And when it comes to great wines the disparity is even more marked. In the Médoc Ch. Margaux, for example, covers 240 acres, and Ch. Lafite 130; while on the Côte d'Or, Chambertin fills only $32\frac{1}{2}$ and Romanée-Conti only $4\frac{1}{2}$!

This may be the place to note that a niggardly year may not be a bad one for quality as well. 1965 was; 1961, on the other hand, which is outside our table but which was considerably smaller even than 1965, was of excellent quality. I should perhaps also remark that, even with low-yielding figures such as those of 1969 and 1967 in it, my table shows a considerably higher average than those given in most text-books on the region. This is because these go further back into history than I do; and, fortunately for us, improved methods of viticulture are steadily increasing output, whenever the weather does not interfere too violently.

However, for the average of the last five years, if no one else in the world drank burgundy (which unhappily is not the fact), there would still be less than six bottles per head per year for the population of the British Isles – men, women and children. True, not many children drink burgundy, and not so many women; still these figures do explain the demand and price here, quite apart from the requirements of all the other greedy nationals who are after this wine. For the Americans, even if it all went to the United States, the situation would be worse; they could have little more than a bottle a head per year.

	AC				
	1971	1970	1969 (in cases)	1968	1967
Côte d'Or	1,694,000	3,210,000	2,041,000	2,169,000	1,905,000
Saône-et-Loire (Chalonnais & Mâconnais)	3,541,000	5,187,500	3,185,000	3,967,000	2,405,000
Rhône (Beaujolais)	7,758,500	11,900,000	7,080,000	9,247,500	7,627,000
Yonne (including Chablis)	392,500	782,000	430,500	552,000	506,000
Total Burgundy	13,386,000	21,079,500	12,709,500	15,935,500	12,443,000

	Non-AC				
	1971	1970	1969 (in cases)	1968	1967
Côte d'Or	688,000	1,185,500	826,000	1,205,000	795,500
Saône-et-Loire (Chalonnais & Mâconnais)	1,229,500	1,764,000	1,257,000	1,758,000	1,206,500
Rhône (Beaujolais)	2,520,500	1,386,500	794,000	1,268,000	932,000
Yonne (including Chablis)	335,500	1,316,000	482,000	554,000	719,000
Total Burgundy	4,773,500	5,652,000	3,359,000	4,785,000	3,653,000

This gives a five-year average of 15,110,700 cases of *AC* and 4,444,500 of non-*AC*, with 1970 a superabundant year for both, and 1969 and 1967 meagre ones. The table also shows the variations of output in the different districts, as they are affected by the local rigours of the climate.

The situation is even worse if one takes only the production of the best fields of the Côte d'Or, the archetypal burgundy. In 1966, a prolific year, outside the above table, the *grands* and 1st *crus* of this *département* yielded the meagre total of 119,000 cases of red and 25,000 of white. The lesser wines of this finest area, technically called '*villages*' – i.e., minor single-vineyard and *commune* wines, but still good – could only supply a further 1,347,000 cases of red and 301,000 cases of white. (The differential between this figure and that given for the whole Côte d'Or of 2,865,000 cases is made up by wines with general *appellations* – *bourgogne, bourgogne grand ordinaire* or *ordinaire, passe-tout-grains* and *aligoté* – all of which will be described in greater detail in the next two chapters.) No wonder most of us fall back on the Chalonnais, the Mâconnais and the Beaujolais for our daily drinking.

To compare the output of the four *départements* graphically Monsieur Jean Thorin jr made for me a sketch of a burgundy bottle divided into three sections. If all the wine of Burgundy were poured into it, the Côte d'Or and Chablis would fill the straight neck above the bulge. The Chalonnais and Mâconnais would fill the shoulders. The body of the bottle would be filled by beaujolais.

Although I intend to speak of cases and bottles throughout the book, I suppose the Burgundian trade measures ought to be quoted. They are not of much importance to the ordinary British or American drinker, but they may be seen in further reading and be confusing if not recorded here. In terms of the Côte d'Or, then, a *queue* of wine equals 456 litres, or 608 bottles. I say 'equals', because this is only a measure, as barrels of this capacity are not actually used. The common hogshead, half a *queue*, is called a *pièce*, of 228 litres or 304 bottles. The half-hogshead, of 152 bottles is a *feuillette*, and the quarter, of 76 bottles, is a *quarteau*. However, if you are going to import wholesale and do your own bottling, as Robert Speaight does among other English Burgundophils, you should be advised that the capacity of these measures varies from one part of Burgundy to another. In Chablis the commonly-used *feuillette* is larger than on the Côte d'Or, and in the Mâconnais and

Beaujolais all the measures are smaller. It would be tedious to give the details, but if you are buying in French containers you must check the precise number of litres they hold.

In any event the effective output in bottles is smaller, when allowance has been made for wastage. A Côte d'Or *pièce* will fill from 290 to 300 bottles, probably nearer to the lower figure, particularly with amateur bottling.

The ordinary burgundy bottle of seventy-five centilitres represents about $1\frac{5}{16}$ imperial pints, but there is also a special beaujolais bottle called the *pot*, two thirds the size of the ordinary bottle, and a handy measure, by the way, of seven eighths of a pint. Some of these *pots* are made, especially for the American trade, in attractive shapes; though in general I should be wary of wine, or spirits, put up in fancy containers.

So the general picture of Burgundy is of a comparatively small volume of wine made by an enormous number of producers. True, the very littlest men no longer make their own wine commercially, but sell their grapes to the shippers. (The same phenomenon is beginning to appear in Bordeaux, though tiny vineyards are much less common there.) But the bulk of the owners of even an acre or so still make their own wine, though they have not the capacity nor capital to store it till it is drinkable, nor the equipment to bottle it. They bottle a little for their own family consumption, but otherwise sell in hogsheads to the shippers, who are responsible for maturing and selling the wine. Over 80% of burgundy passes through the hands of the shippers. Some of these make wine from their own *AC* vineyards also, but this element represents a small fraction only of the total trade. Probably 90% of the wine sold by the shippers has been originally made by small independent proprietors.

All this explains why Burgundy has been described as 'the democracy of wine'. I accept this description if it is taken objectively, without any implication of intrinsic merit. In the nineteenth century Anglo-Saxons and many Western European countries accepted 'democracy' as the ideal political organization. It is losing repute politically, and has long been abandoned as the optimum in industry and agriculture.

The fragmentation of ownership has however one good consequence; it breeds a large number not of specialized employés but of free masters who know the whole of their honourable if laborious craft. Hence that fine independence of character and notable individualism that every traveller in Burgundy must remark among the proprietors. Four hundred years ago Erasmus said, 'Burgundy may well be called the mother of men, having such noble milk within her breasts to suckle her sons.' This independence reaches its apogee among the small proprietors. Ownership of a Burgundian vineyard is something like a patent of nobility, even if most of the fiefs are minuscule.

But the system is, economically, undeniably inefficient. Further, the larger the flock, the larger, potentially, the number of its black sheep. From this 'democracy' spring some of the fraudulent practices against which we must be on guard. Small men are liable to temptations that larger businesses resist, not necessarily because of the higher morality of the people involved, but because of the importance of safeguarding vast investments. The *société anonyme* is really far less anonymous than the small proprietor. Honesty is certainly the best policy, to put it no higher, for the big shipper. Those who depart from it soon get known to the experienced buyer, and then years of established goodwill are lost.

Now the worst potential results of this fragmentation of ownership are offset by the intermediaries known as *courtiers*, or brokers, who handle almost all the sales – perhaps 90% of the entire trade – of the proprietors to the shippers. Some writers have denigrated these brokers, just because they are middlemen, and add to the cost of merchandising. But they serve a most useful purpose in the industry in reconnoitring the small-holdings and introducing their products to the shippers. They are helpful also to the merchants overseas who like to buy direct from the grower – and who thereby often get very interesting wine at a very economical price. They are the descendants of the old *dégustateurs-jurés*, by whose verdicts law-suits were settled in the Middle Ages, and are of very ancient lineage.

No big shipper can possibly deal with all the multiplicity of growers. But the broker makes this his business. At any rate in one section of the field he knows every proprietor, and particularly every *maître du chai*. Some of the leaders even cover the whole of Burgundy; others specialize in the Chalonnais, the Mâconnais, the Beaujolais and Chablis. They are familiar with the style of wine wanted by each shipper for whom they work on commission, and can guide him to it.

As soon as the proprietor has made his wine the broker tastes it and recommends it to suitable buyers. When it is ready for delivery he tests it again. After delivery the shipper has a week in which to reject the wine before putting it into his cellar. In case of dispute the broker acts as arbiter. This is a responsible function, for wine rejected can only be sold for vinegar, at a fraction of the price it would otherwise have realized.

The broker is not needed, of course, for famous vineyards, though his services are often utilized even there. But for *commune* wine he handles nearly every transaction. His work might not seem to be of interest to the reader of such a work as this, but in reality these gentlemen are of great importance to the retail buyer. They have remarkable expertise, and use this to help maintain the quality and style of the wine we drink.

Still, for all their efforts, the unevenness of quality and character that is the common count against burgundy cannot be eliminated. There will always be differences, because sites, even in the same *commune*, vary markedly in their elevation and orientation. Further, with thousands of small owners at work the bunches will have been picked on different days, and with different levels of scrupulosity in eliminating inferior grapes. The care in *égrappage* (the separation of grapes from stems) and in avoiding the crushing of the pips in the presses will have varied. Even the cleanliness of some vats may have left something to be desired. Certainly the speed and duration of the fermentation will have been different from parcel to parcel, and there are other factors of inconsistency that it would be tiresome to enumerate. The skilful shipper will do his best to overcome these vagaries by blending; but perfect reliability is hard to achieve.

It is true that such differentia must prevail in all *commune* wines in all wine-producing areas, but they are appreciably increased in Burgundy by this extreme exiguity of the average vineyard. In the Beaujolais a number of cooperatives have been formed to deal with the problems of the small producer; but cooperatives are uncommon elsewhere in Burgundy. More perhaps would be desirable, but the traditions of Burgundy are against it, at any rate on the Côte d'Or. There is even an official organization whose initials are SAFER, whose purpose is to prevent consolidation. It must approve all sales of vineyards, and uses this power not only, desirably, to keep outsiders with no knowledge from cashing in on the prestige of vineyard-ownership, but also, more questionably, to prevent large proprietors taking over small ones, and so creating anything like a local monopoly.

Even a famous vineyard like Clos Vougeot, which is the biggest enclosure of the Côte d'Or (125 acres), and which ought to produce one of the most integrated of burgundies, is known by every experienced drinker to be remarkably variegated. For there are some sixty owners with plots in those 125 acres, and though they represent the cream of Burgundy ownership both their methods and skills are still different, and the level of their vineyards also. I once met a man who claimed to be able to tell by blind tasting the elevation at which the grapes had been grown on the slopes of this *clos*. But if this was true, I do not think that even he could have spotted the individual vintner.

Let us ignore, for the time being, the deliberate misuse of names, which is by no means confined, as French chauvinists have claimed, to British bottling. (This will be covered in Chapter 15.) Let us assume that everything has been done perfectly legitimately. Even so it requires the finest skill of the best shippers to overcome the different starts that *commune* wines have had. So we get that lack of uniformity that I had to refer to, right at the beginning, in my Preface. This is sometimes the despair of the commencing drinker who is attentive to his different bottles, and a matter of fascinated interest to the more experienced.

The champions of claret assert, with fair reason, that in a given year every bottle of a given *château*, providing it has been properly transported and cellared, will taste the same. This is only strictly true of château-bottled wine, since the resources, skill and traditions of Bordeaux shippers vary as do those of their *confrères* elsewhere. And even with a château-bottled wine not all the grapes of a given vineyard will have been picked on the same day, in the same weather. The vintage of 1964 is a notorious example, when rain started in the middle of the picking. Nevertheless what the Bordelais claim is largely true.

Leaving on one side the great classified *châteaux*, different bottlings of a *cru bourgeois* of claret, perhaps even a *cru artisan*, of 1966, say, whether done in Bordeaux or Britain, will, given equal skill and treatment, be virtually alike. But to go back to our instance of Clos Vougeot: two bottles of 1966 sold by different shippers, even if both have been bottled in Nuits or Beaune, will be as different, not as chalk from cheese but as white Cheshire from pink Cheshire, though each is genuinely entitled to be called Clos Vougeot. (The ones bottled in some distinguished cellars in Britain, be it said in passing, may well be better than those bottled in Burgundy.) Hence the caution, which wine-writers repeat *ad nauseam* perhaps, but *ex necessitate*, of knowing your shipper, and the ultimate merchant, when you are buying burgundy.

It is not of course essential that the shipper should blend only wines from one *commune*. A skilled cellar-master can sometimes achieve better results by mixing wines from different *communes*. This is perfectly legitimate provided the product is sold as *bourgogne*, and not by a *commune* name.

All these problems have caused extreme dissatisfaction to some of my friends in the United States, who have a fine taste for wine but cannot call on the services of the numerous distinguished merchants whose guidance we still enjoy in Great Britain. Buying in America is therefore being more and more concentrated on single-vineyard burgundies, to which I shall go on to refer. But there is also the protection of the half-way house – that of the burgundy shipper bottling *commune* wines from his own vineyards, whether single-vineyards or not, under the title of *Mise du Domaine* or with the label *Mis en bouteilles au Domaine* or *Mise de la Propriété*. Here the same firm has grown, made and bottled the product, and consistency may be expected, within the inevitable variations of different years. But it still does not carry the same guarantee as a château-bottled wine of Bordeaux. It may be the *mise* of the *Domaine*, but it is not *mis* at the *Domaine*. The cellars of the shippers are mostly in the bigger towns. Wines produced by the shipper of the same *appellation*, from his own vines, will still have been affected by methods of transport, weather and other factors.

Some of the sharper dealers, by the way, try to bemuse the innocent by putting on their labels such words as *Mis en bouteilles dans nos caves*. This means nothing. Every bottler bottles in his cellars. The question is, what does he put into the bottles? Also I am not impressed by the new trick of using portable bottling plants, going from property to property, so that almost any wine can claim to be *domaine*-bottled.

So finally the purist is forced back, if he wants the best and most authentic, to what I have said American connoisseurs demand and all reasonably well-off drinkers in Britain choose for special occasions; single-vineyard wines. Here you have the ultimate security of similarity of style that can be given by anything so organic, so alive, and hence so mutable, as wine.

Having spent so much as you will have to for a single-vineyard wine of great repute, I suppose it is sensible to pay the little more for Burgundy bottling; though even with these single-vineyard wines I have tasted samples bottled in Bristol and London against those bottled in Burgundy, and have found them indistinguishable except for the more modest price of the British bottling.

Fortunately a taste for single-vineyard wines does not involve always paying the price of *grand crus*. There are splendid 1st *crus* that are noble drinking in any decent year; and no reasonable man would complain about having to put up, most of the while, with the lesser single-vineyard wines that are technically known as *Villages* but may show their own name after that of their *commune*. Indeed, for the discriminating drinker who must seriously consider price, these perhaps offer the best value. The ranking of these named *crus* will be explained in Chapter 4.

But while each single vineyard retains its style, there is still an engrossing variety among the fine named vineyards from the same *commune*. I once drank two wines together at the Vintners' Hall, a Beaune Theurons and a Beaune Grèves, each of the somewhat undervalued year 1948. The first had a bouquet of warm fruit in a walled garden; the second offered to the nose no suggestion of fruity acidity, but only a kind of ethereal sweetness. The taste of the first was luscious, almost perfumed, and the texture seemed weighted, as if it had more than the specific gravity of wine; the second, on the other hand, had a forthright savour, and the wine, despite its age, seemed active and working. Each, needless to say, had been well cellared.

However, I have now been led into the subject of the grading of burgundy. This requires a chapter to itself, but I think it will be clearer if, before tackling the grades, I say something of the grapes.

Still, before this I had better refer to another element of confusion in the Burgundian system. Everybody knows about it, but not everybody can draw the necessary deductions. I am speaking of the practice of *communes* hitching their names onto those of their famous vineyards. It is like the undistinguished man in England who marries a landed heiress and hyphenates her name with his; thus plain Mr Smith, after his lucky coup, becomes Smith-Cholmondely, Esq. So the ordinary village of Gevrey adopted the extraordinary Chambertin area, Chambolle adopted Musigny, Flagey adopted Echézeaux, Vosne adopted Romanée, Nuits adopted St-Georges, and both Puligny and Chassagne climbed on board the fabulous wagon of Montrachet. The process went so far that Pernand was glad to be hitched onto Vergelesses and Auxey onto Duresses, though in these cases the second names only included 1st *cru* vineyards and no *grands crus*.

Only Beaune, Pommard, Volnay, Meursault and Santenay have maintained their independence, so to speak, together with the minor *communes* of Fixin, Monthélie and a few others; and even so Savigny horned into a part of Beaune and elevated itself into Savigny-les-Beaune. Clos Vougeot was big enough to be a law unto itself; the neighbouring village of Gilly once tried to be ennobled as Gilly-les-Vougeot, but could not maintain this pretension.

Now the implication was that all the double-barrelled *communes* absorbed the quality of the greatest vineyards within their area. This is not a fact. They inherited some of the prestige, but there the comparison generally ends, though I suppose it is broadly true that the hyphenated communes rank, one against another, in about the order that skilled judgement would allocate to the great names to which they have linked themselves.

However, the beginner must not think that even the finest shipper's Vosne-Romanée will be the next thing to Romanée-Conti. It won't. It will be wine made from vineyards near (often right next to) the finest, and echoing something of its character, but only with such guarantee of quality as the area's reputation (and the shipper's integrity) implies.

So the burgundy trade, with which I have been dealing, consists of growers (mostly very small), brokers, shippers, merchants – in countries with a proper selling organization – and in some a State monopoly, which I should not consider a proper selling organization. Each area also has its trade association, and over all there is a professional supervisory body. I have listed some quarrels with them. But on the whole, to all, though they have their weaknesses, we should be duly grateful for the labour and skill that ends, most often, in the delight of our palates.

3. The Grapes of Burgundy

I have disclaimed the intention of writing a technical book. However, to understand the qualities of burgundy it is necessary to know something of the grapes of which it is generally composed; but we can pass over the uncommon permitted varieties which are of slight importance.

All good burgundy then, except beaujolais, is made of the *pinot* family, low of yield but high in esteem. The red comes from the *pinot noir fin*, generally abbreviated to *pinot noir*. The white comes from the *pinot blanc*, or *chardonnay*.

The *pinot noir* is also known as the *pinot noirien*; and to a small extent the *pinot Beurot* and *pinot Liebault* are used in the making of superior red wine. Some people further confuse the issue by using the alternative spelling, in some or all cases, of *pineau*. But for the common drinker, it is sufficient to know that his choice red burgundy – other, as I have said, than beaujolais – is made of the *pinot noir*.

Tiny admixtures of the juice of other grapes is permitted by *AC* rules for *commune* wines, but in general you may say that the high-yielding *gamay* is ruled out for better red burgundy made north of the Mâconnais. When the *gamay* is used in ordinary burgundy the bottle must be labelled as *bourgogne passe-tout-grains*. The general proportion is then two-thirds *gamay* to one-third *pinot noir*.

It is, incidentally, interesting to get a bottle of this and compare it at an informal tasting with a genuine *pinot noir* bottle of not too high a quality, say a *bourgogne*. The difference is immediately obvious. Yet the *passe-tout-grains* has a certain earthy (some people say, bodily) flavour that is not unattractive. When it sails under its own true and modest colours *passe-tout-grains* is an acceptable cheap drink which I find preferable to *corsé* red wines of similar price coming from other areas.

Now no book on burgundy would be complete without a reference to the famous edict of Philip the Bold of 1395 forbidding the use in Burgundy of the '*très mauvais et très desloyaux plant nommé gamay*'. The violence of this old denunciation of the *gamay*, which in the Beaujolais produces good to excellent wine, has suggested to some writers that the Duke was fulminating not against the true *gamay*, which is the *gamay noir à jus blanc*, but against its inferior cousin the *gamay à jus coloré*, or *gamay teinturier*. This is still held in general disrepute, and even in the Beaujolais must never exceed 10% by volume of any *AC* wine.

But I have found no historical authority for this surmise. I think it is much more likely that the breed of the *gamay* has been improved since its old outlawry. The excellence of its product in the Beaujolais can hardly be entirely due to the granitic soil of that area. We know of numerous fruits that have been vastly improved in recorded horticultural history. Why may not the plebeian *gamay* have benefited by the technique of the breeders? (Within recent years the size and regularity of the shape of the *pinot noir* has been noticeably increased.) Which is not meant in the least to suggest that the *gamay* can be compared with the aristocratic *pinot noir* for the limestone soil of the Côte d'Or.

The noble grape for white burgundy is the *pinot blanc* or *chardonnay*, which is sometimes called the *pinot blanc vrai*. Various authorities write of the *pinot blanc chardonnay*, of *pinot chardonnay*, and of *pinot-chardonnay* (only most of them start these names with capitals). To get a ruling I applied to André Simon, then the greatest authority in this country on French wine-grapes. He wrote to me (28 November 1966):

Pinot or Pineau is the name of a large family of *cépages nobles noirs et blancs*.

Le Chardonnay is the normal way of referring to the most popular white member of the family, in Burgundy, by the *vignerons* and the trade.

Pinot Blanc is the first cousin of the Chardonnay, which is usually called the Pinot Blanc vrai. Pinot Blanc Chardonnay and Pinot Chardonnay cannot be said to be false or 'wrong' descriptions, since the Chardonnay is both a Pinot and Pinot white, but I am in favour of using 'Chardonnay' by itself, as they do in Bourgogne. The hyphen (Pinot-Chardonnay) is distinctly wrong.

The oracle has spoken. For this book the fine white grape of Burgundy shall be the *chardonnay*, as the name of *pinot noir* has been selected for our purposes for its red brother.

In Chablis the *chardonnay* has a local name of *beaunois*. It is a very small producer on that chalky soil. Its use is not required in petit chablis, which may be made of any reputable grape providing the alcoholic strength does not fall below 9·5°.

Now in white burgundy the common poor cousin (the equivalent of the *gamay* for red burgundy other than that of the southern areas) is the prolific *aligoté*, of which most ordinary whites are made and whose name should appear on the label of all *AC* wines for which it is employed.

To a small extent the *gamay blanc*, also known as the *melon de Bourgogne*, is used for inexpensive wines in southern Burgundy, but we need not bother about it for the Côte d'Or, the home of the great wines. Incidentally I think the *aligoté* makes a better white wine on the Côte d'Or than the *gamay* makes a red. There is an attractive freshness about, for example, Avery's Puligny *aligoté* that I keep as one of my table wines at home when (as usual nowadays) I am economizing. It is a little acid, but an unpretentious drink that goes well with the coarser fish and the *assiette anglaise* of Sunday supper, and very good value for the money. You should always be suspicious of the *gamay* except – I keep having to repeat this – in the Beaujolais: you need never be suspicious of the *aligoté*. It is an honest second-rater.

There seems to be much confusion among the 'authorities' about the grape used for white beaujolais (see Chapter 10). It is commonly stated to be the *aligoté*, and I believe this was true when the making of white beaujolais was confined to the south of the area. But most of the good white beaujolais that is shipped now, certainly nearly all that is exported, comes from the northern part of the area, near the famous Pouilly-Fuissé *appellation* in the Mâconnais. Indeed, until the recent staggering growth in the popularity of beaujolais, most of this wine was sold as mâcon *blanc*. And for this, though the *AC* rules tolerate *aligoté*, the *chardonnay* is more and more used.

The most thorough research into this question that I have seen was made by S. P. E. Simon for some articles in the *Wine and Spirit Trade Review*. In this he says positively that if you want a beaujolais *aligoté* you will have to look for it, not in the lists of the export shippers, still less in the catalogues of British merchants, but at the bars of cafés down in the Lyonnais and in the carafes of little bistros in the city of Lyon itself.

To sum up: ignoring unimportant exceptions, red burgundy on the Côte d'Or and in the Chalonnais is made of the *pinot noir*; if the *gamay* is used you should be warned by the label *passe-tout-grains*. In the Mâconnais the *gamay* makes acceptable red wine. In the Beaujolais the *gamay* makes good red wine, and the *pinot noir* is forbidden for the finest growths. Fine white wine, everywhere in Burgundy, is made of the *chardonnay*; for ordinary wine, if the *aligoté* is used, this should be stated on the label.

The difference between wine made of 'noble' growths and of others is of course finally distinguished on the palate. But before that stage the yield is the criterion. The niggardly grape produces fine wine, the prolific grape ordinary wine. Even so, things are not left to nature; there are, for Burgundy, as indeed for all French wines, certain rules concerning productivity. On the Côte d'Or for fine vineyards the original *AC* regulations grant the *pinot* and the *chardonnay* a maximum permitted yield, in round figures, of 1600 bottles per acre, and for *commune* vineyards (as also for the best *crus* of the Chalonnais) of 1875. The latter figure is the permitted maximum for the *grands crus* of Chablis, while chablis 1st *crus*, chablis and petit chablis can make up to 2170 bottles per acre. In the Chalonnais *communes* the *pinot* may also be stretched to the last figure. And even the fine *chardonnay crus* of Pouilly-Fuissé can produce up to 2415 bottles per acre, which is one of the principal reasons why they rarely rank with the great white wines of the Côte Beaune.

The *gamay* on the other hand may yield up to 2170 bottles per acre – the same as for chablis, or mere petit chablis – even in the fine *crus* of the Beaujolais; up to 2415 in beaujolais *Villages* and beaujolais *supérieur*; and up to 2710 in beaujolais *ordinaire*. But on the Côte d'Or even the *gamay* is not allowed to go as far as this. There, mixed two for one with the *pinot*, the top permitted yield for *passe-tout-grains* is only 2435 bottles per acre – as it is also for *bourgogne*, made of *pinot* alone, which shows how far the *pinot* could go if permitted.

These figures, as I have said, are maxima under *AC* rules. However, the normal yield of all grapes, with the improved methods of modern viticulture, is increasing steadily. Therefore when these maxima are applied to prolific vintages, excellent wine is condemned to be sold, at markedly lower prices, as *bourgogne*. The wine is officially 'declassified'; for example, excess production of Clos Vougeot can be sold as *bourgogne* only. Which, it is felt, is absurd. So in prolific years the *AC* administration extends the permitted yields by about 5% to 10%, and sometimes even more, above the strict maxima – *but only after a tasting in each case by a committee of impartial experts*, who must assure themselves that the larger output has not resulted in a lessening of quality. In the exceptional year of 1970 the permitted excess of the fine vineyards was increased very substantially. So consumers of this precious merchandise 'in short supply' are marginally protected against the rigours of legalism.

Still, it must be remembered that the maxima are gross, before any loss by evaporation or in racking. So that the actual amount of wine of each class, per acre, that reaches the bottles we drink is in fact less than the figures set out above, even if and when they are increased by the authorities.

But whatever the grape and whatever the yield, you will note, as you go through Burgundy, the conscientious care with which even the humblest vineyards are tended. At every season some laborious task is being performed – some of them, which cannot be mechanized, almost back-breaking. The vines are well spaced, just over a metre apart, not only to facilitate cultivation and spraying against fungi and parasites, but also to set quality above output; but not too widely, because, curiously enough, this not only results in still lower output but also in inferior fruit. Everything is done as the result of centuries of experience, and when new machines are introduced, the tractors for example, their measurements are designed to accommodate this traditional spacing.

The vines are severely pruned, and as the shoots form these are dressed low. Later the number of bunches is reduced to the optimum for quality. Meanwhile the ground is continuously cultivated (in the farmer's sense of that word), but not deeply, as this would bring up the infertile sub-soil. Manuring, principally with potassium, is also carefully regulated, as excessive fertilization would produce unfortunate tastes in the juices. The vines are never watered; nature provides enough moisture in this climate, and irrigation is undesirable because wet roots produce grapes swollen with water and lacking in alcoholic potentiality.

The year of the grape may be summarily described by the following calendar. In October the stripped vineyards are trenched and refertilized. In November the soil is cultivated, and replaced where there has been erosion. In December this work is continued, and pruning begins, which is carried on into January and February. For this work experienced craftsmen are still required; the general mechanization of viticulture cannot, as yet, eliminate personal skill and judgement for this crucial task.

In March the pruning is reaching its end. Meanwhile the tilled soil is ploughed back, and in the nurseries new vines are grafted onto phylloxera-resistant roots for future production. All of the plants now, since even Romanée-Conti has had to dig up its *vieilles vignes*, are grafted onto American roots as a safeguard against phylloxera, the deadliest of the vine's many diseases. Hybrid vines are forbidden.

In April grafts of previous years are planted out, and established vines are trained to the lowest wires of the cordons. In May the planting continues, while vineyards in production are treated against diseases, for which agricultural advisory services provide instructions. The traditional, picturesque copper sulphate spray, for better or worse, has been largely replaced by synthetic prophylactics.

June sees the continuation of May's procedure, and the vines – again with the advice of the consultancy service – are appropriately treated with sulphur against the deadly oidium. In July sulphate is added to the sulphur, and the vines are scraped and topped. In August the final touches are given to the vines, baskets are repaired, and in the *cuvage* chambers all presses, vats and hosepipes are cleansed, and pumps retested.

Finally, usually near the end of September, comes the vintage. The old *ban de vendange*, fixed for each *commune* by duly constituted local authorities, calculated on traditional intervals from the flowering of the vines, has now been replaced by individual initiative on the advice of oenological stations, given after scientific tests. On this the cutters begin their work – generally between 20 September and 19 October. Women in white headdresses carry the grapes to men clad in long aprons, who carry the heavy accumulations of the *pinots*, *chardonnays* and so forth. Each *côte* has different traditional containers.

The apogee of the vine-year, the vintage, is a wonderful spectacle. It is a scene of vigorous but ordered activity. The sense of being engaged in a task both economically important and socially beneficent gives spirit to the workers; and if everything has been favourable – an early flowering, enough rain in summer, sun in August and a dry autumn with the consequent late harvest – then the sense of a fine year produces infectious gaiety among the workers, even imported townspeople or students. And the hearts of the *vignerons* rejoice over the successful outcome, after their long cycle of anxieties concerning the vagaries of the weather and the continuous threat of pests.

4. The Grades of Burgundy

The finest burgundies, red and white, are all single-vineyard wines. At the top of the list come a few *grands crus* or *têtes de cuvée* – for example, Romanée-Conti or Le Montrachet – which need not use their *commune* names, but stand by themselves. Then there are a larger number of 1st *crus* or 1st *cuvées* – such as Chambolle-Musigny Les Amoureuses and Puligny-Montrachet Les Caillerets. And there are, according to some authorities, who do not however all agree on their grading of various vineyards, a yet larger number of 2nd and 3rd *crus* or *cuvées*. All below the first grand category must state their *commune* names on the label.

Next come the *commune* wines (for example, Gevrey-Chambertin) made from various vineyards within a single *commune*, whose name they bear without any vineyard specification. If some of these are made entirely from 1st *cru* vineyards they may be described as, e.g., Morey-St-Denis *premier cru*. Such shipments are rare on the Côte d'Or, but fairly common in Chablis, where the tiny output of the 1st *cru* vineyards often makes it necessary to mingle the juice of two or more to make a shipment of commercial size. A chablis 1st *cru*, naturally, will rank above a simple chablis.

A number of the minor *communes* of the Côte de Nuits – part of Fixin, Brochon, Prissey, Comblanchien and Corgoloin – are permitted to sell their wine as Vins Fins de la Côte de Nuits, or Côte de Nuits-Villages.

Similarly the Côte de Beaune has minor *commune* classifications, Côtes de Beaune and Côtes de Beaune Villages. The grapes of the former can come not only from the Beaune area properly so called, but also from a small exterior acreage; the

the latter is a blending of at least two minor fields adjacent to the main Beaune area. Côtes de Beaune can be red or white, but is mostly red; Côtes de Beaune Villages is all red. These wines should be modestly priced, and are often good purchases for ordinary drinking, as they are not important enough to fake – as is a good deal of Beaune *commune* wine that comes into our market.

Next in quality after the *commune* wines comes *bourgogne*. This may be made of grapes from any area within the specified vineyards of Burgundy, providing they are *pinot noir* for the red (or *gamay* for mâconnais and beaujolais) and *chardonnay* for the white. This *bourgogne*, made in a good year and shipped by a reliable shipper, is often excellent value, because it may consist of *commune* (or even single-vineyard) wines that have been made in excess of the amount permitted by the regulations, and so deprived of the *AC* label for its *commune* or field. Thus it becomes what is technically called 'declassified' into *bourgogne*. But of course most *bourgogne* is of humbler origin. Your palate must be the judge – though personally I find it safer to get an expert merchant to advise me.

Then comes *bourgogne grand ordinaire*, or *bourgogne ordinaire*. (They are the same thing.) It is important to remember that this ranks below *bourgogne* without any addition to the name. It has a lower alcoholic strength than *bourgogne*, so may not travel so well, and may contain percentages of *gamay* grapes in the red and *aligoté* in the white.

Finally there are *passe-tout-grains*, made of two-thirds *gamay* and one-third *pinot*; and *bourgogne aligoté*, made (obviously) of *aligoté* grapes, though it may have a small balancing factor of the better *chardonnay*.

To sum up, this is the table of precedence:

1. Single-vineyard *grands crus* or *têtes de cuvée*
2. Single-vineyard *premiers crus* or *premières cuvées*
3. Single-vineyard 2nd or 3rd *crus* or 2nd or 3rd *cuvées* (but see later, pages 48–50)

4. *Commune* wines
5. Vins fin de la Côte de Nuits, or Côte de Nuits-Villages
6. (for Beaune only) (a) Côtes de Beaune,
                      (b) Côtes de Beaune Villages
7. *Bourgogne*
8. *Bourgogne grand ordinaire*, or *bourgogne ordinaire*
9. *Passe-tout-grains* (red) and *aligoté* (white).

For Chablis the table of precedence is:
1. Chablis *grand cru* (usually from a single vineyard)
2. Chablis *premier cru* (often from a single vineyard)
3. Chablis
4. Petit chablis

These chablis *appellations* will be discussed in more detail in Chapter 11; and the chalonnais, mâconnais and beaujolais classifications in Chapters 9 and 10. There are also classifications of *bourgogne rosé* (or *clairet*) and *bourgogne mousseux*, which will be covered in Chapter 13. In all there are 114 controlled *appellations* of burgundy, so it will be seen that some simplification is necessary in a book of this size.

Now I have spoken of '*grands crus* or *têtes de cuvée*' and so on down to '3rd *crus* or 3rd *cuvées*' for single-vineyard wines. Which is the more correct, *cru* or *cuvée*? – since considerations of space, if not also of style, forbid the repetitions of these alternatives. And in either case, how many grades of them are there?

The original Burgundian classification of 1861, based on a minute examination of the vineyards and a close study of tradition, but not claiming other authority, divided the vineyards into three 'classes'. It is substantially on this basis that the vineyards are still mapped in the authoritative *Atlas Larmat*, coloured pink for 1st class, yellow for 2nd class and deep green for 3rd class. It will be noted how the pink fields on the Côte d'Or follow the middle slopes (on the contoured maps) everywhere except at Clos Vougeot (whence the variability of this *appellation*) and at the minor *communes* of Premeaux and Prissey. The contours of the pink areas run from about 750 to 1,000 feet above sea-level, which is about 75 to 325 feet above the Saône. They are sheltered by higher fields to the west. It must also be remembered that a 3rd class single vineyard produces 1st class wine in any common acceptance of that phrase; but not such fine wine as a 2nd class vineyard.

There are also pale green vineyards in this indispensable guide that have a right to *commune appellation*, and also still less important ones in grey; but both of these colours introduce complications that need not trouble us, for their wines are not exported under their individual names.

Now the famous Burgundian, Camille Rodier, co-founder of the *Confrérie des Chevaliers du Tastevin*, took over, in his book *Le Vin de Bourgogne*, these 1861 classifications but divided them into *cuvées* of various degree; *têtes de cuvée*, 1st, 2nd and 3rd *cuvées*. Our P. Morton Shand, in *A Book of French Wines* (recently revised by Cyril Ray), adopted a similar classification. So did Alexis Lichine in his *Wines of France*. André Simon, in his own chapter of the recent *Wines of the World* that he edited, lists a number of *têtes de cuvée*, and refers to 1st, 2nd and 3rd *cuvées*. The authors agreed generally, but by no means completely, as to which were *têtes*, 1st, 2nd and 3rd.

Louis Jacquelin's and René Poulain's *Vignes et Vins de France* recognized, though again with some personal variations, the quadruple ranking, but, to increase our difficulties, sometimes called them *crus* and sometimes *cuvées*.

Meanwhile, from 1938 on there appeared the revised, presumably improved, and certainly official *AC* classification, based on the *Décret-Loi* of 1935. This used the word *cru* instead of *cuvée*, and recognized only *grands crus* and 1st *crus*. The elaborate tables of 2nd and 3rd *crus*, perhaps through commercial pressure, were all lumped together. All vineyards not recognized by the *appellation* as *grands* or 1st *crus* became simply *Villages*.

Les Vins du Bourgogne, by Pierre Poupon and Pierre Forgeot, followed the official *AC* classification, called the single vineyards *crus*, and accepted only *grand crus* and 1st *crus*.

When I was in Burgundy before writing this book I discussed these problems of nomenclature and classification with these gentlemen – Monsieur Poupon is technical director of the Beaune house of Calvet and Monsieur Forgeot is general secretary of the *Syndicat des Négociants en vins de Bourgogne* – and with numerous proprietors, brokers and shippers, not to mention an oenologist or two. All were agreed that *cru* is the proper word to apply to a vineyard, and *cuvée* to the wine. And it is the location of the vineyard that, year in, year out, determines the quality of the wine. *Cuvée*, it was said, is an indeterminate word with no official standing. According to one of the informants, any little proprietor of a pale green or even grey vineyard in the *Atlas* who makes a good wine in a fortunate year could call it his *tête de cuvée*. *Cru* is an objective word, *cuvée* is a subjective one; the former a fact, the latter an opinion.

In the face of this current unanimity I feel I must use the word *cru*, of the *AC* regulations, though the reader should understand that my *grands crus* and 1st *crus* are other authors' *têtes de cuvée* and 1st *cuvées*. (In Chablis, by the way, everyone has always called them *crus*.) Similarly, to avoid cluttering my text with vineyard names, few of which are known in international trade, I shall mention only *grands crus* and the best-known 1st *crus* in the body of the book. But I shall add an appendix (B, pages 192 to 202) setting out all the *grands* and 1st *crus* accepted by the *Atlas Larmat* and Poupon and Forgeot's book. This avoids the invidious distinctions introduced by others. However, in my Epilogue I shall temerariously offer my own ranking of the *grands crus* and the best of the 1st, divided into three classes. If I differ from the experts who have already made such classifications it must be remembered that this is a personal book – and also that vineyards have their rises and falls.

The classified *crus* of Chablis, the Chalonnais, the Mâconnais and Beaujolais are few enough to be listed in their respective chapters, though each of these areas has many single vineyards known locally, but too numerous and not sufficiently important in international trade to be mentioned in a book of this scope. However, for ready reference I also set out in Appendix D the *crus* of these fields.

This aforementioned scope prevents me going into minute distinctions within vineyards, where officially one plot may be given one classification, another another. For example, at Nuits-St-Georges the 1st *cru appellation* in the vineyard of Hauts Pruliers is confined to plots 466 to 473, and 534 to 539. The rest are just *Villages*. But if any part of a vineyard is given a certain rank I shall, for brevity, accept the whole vineyard as being of that rank; since under *AC* rules only wine coming from the approved parcels will be sold as, e.g., a 1st *cru*.

After all this discussion of *crus* and *cuvées* it may be asked why, with my preference for English words, I cannot call them 'growths'. And indeed 1st growths (and if admitted, 2nd growths and 3rd growths) would read easily. But what about *grands crus*? 'Exceptional growths'? The French is shorter. 'Superior growths'? But all single-vineyard wines are superior. Let me stick, for simplicity, brevity and official approval, to the French *crus*.

Now how do the *grands crus* of Burgundy compare with the official list of the Médoc (plus Haut-Brion)? Certainly the *grands crus* of Burgundy rank with the 1st *crus* of Bordeaux. The number of them is much greater, but the average output per name very much less.

I doubt however whether even the stoutest champion of Burgundy would assert that all of its 1st *crus* have the distinction of 2nd *cru* clarets. Certainly the 2nd and 3rd red *crus* of burgundy (according to the tables of Rodier and others) are not the equivalents of 2nd and 3rd *crus* of claret. A 2nd *cru* burgundy might be the equivalent of a 4th *cru* claret, but more likely of a 5th *cru*. (Remember that a 5th classified *cru* of bordeaux is an extremely fine wine.) A 3rd *cru* burgundy probably ranks with the best *crus bourgeois supérieurs* of the Médoc or one of the minor *crus* of St Emilion and Pomerol. These 3rd *crus* of burgundy listed in the other books represent vineyards good enough to be shipped as single products, but they are not commonly exported to Great Britain or the United States. On the other hand the 1st *crus* of white burgundy, not to mention the white *grands crus*, rank above anything that Bordeaux or any other field can produce in dry white table wine.

It should however be made clear that all Côte d'Or 1st *crus*, apart from the different characteristics of the *communes* from which they come (which will be discussed in more detail in Chapters 7 and 8) are not of the same quality. Much depends on the general excellence of the *commune*. Thus the northernmost Côte d'Or *commune*, Fixin, has a 1st *cru* (which some critics indeed unofficially classify as a *grand cru*), La Perrière. It is a fine wine, and usually a good buy, since it does not command a very high price. But few would claim that it ranks with such 1st *crus* of the superlative *commune* of Vosne-Romanée as Malconsorts or Suchots.

So if you are in the fortunate position of being able to buy single-vineyard wines, it is not enough to know your lists of *crus*; you must know the respective standing of the various *communes* also; and not only their standings, but also their characteristics. For example, most red wines of the Côte de Beaune are lighter than those of the Côte de Nuits. However, even within the Côte de Nuits, the great *crus* of Chambolle-Musigny, for instance, are much softer than their immediate northern neighbours, the stout growths of Morey-St-Denis. But who shall say whether Musigny (Chambolle-Musigny *commune*) is finer than Clos de Tart (Morey-St-Denis) or vice versa? Here the quality is approximately equal; the preference is a matter of taste.

But of course similar differences exist between the great *crus* of bordeaux. In a given year most judges will agree on the respective merits of a Ch. Lafite and a Ch. Haut-Brion. But over the years your judgement will depend on whether you prefer the characteristics of a Pauillac or a Graves. Incidentally I personally think that the fine burgundies vary less in a given vintage than the fine bordeaux.

It may all sound rather complicated, and perhaps discouraging to the beginner; but with experience and attention (because experience is of little value unless it is attentive), the difficulties will become simplified and the delights more accessible. With burgundy, perhaps more than with most wine, you need to analyse it, discuss it, memorize it, for consistent enjoyment; and discussion helps the memory more than anything else does, more even than reading the authorities, important as that is. The study of wine is a shared enjoyment.

Leaving now the single-vineyard wines, *commune* wines have the greater or lesser distinction both of the *commune* and the shipper. Of these I think the shipper has become on the whole the more important for the quality of the wine. Skill in vinting outweighs the luck of geography, at this level. I should prefer, for quality, a wine made by a scrupulous shipper from a grade B *commune* such as Premeaux to one made by an inferior shipper from a grade A *commune* such as Morey-St-Denis. But for the character of the wine, of course, the *commune* sets the key.

Perhaps I may have seemed to have spoken too disparagingly in Chapter 2 about *commune* wines. There has been much misrepresentation of these, and the past refusal (now under prospect of modification) of the British wine trade to apply the *appellation* rules to their own labelling has led to many disappointments at our tables. But any genuine *commune* wine of the Côte d'Or is already of some distinction. The *AC* rules that have been so painstakingly drawn up for these are generally observed in France. As well as defining the areas, they regulate the grapes used, the output per acre and the minimum alcoholic strength, which together produce excellence.

I noticed that at the lunch at the Élysée that President de Gaulle gave for Messrs Wilson and Brown in January 1967 he just served two *commune* burgundies (before the champagne with the sweet): a Meursault '64 and a Chambolle-Musigny '59.

To take Gevrey-Chambertin as an example: there are eight *grands crus* (of which two, Chambertin and Chambertin-Clos de Bèze, are exceptional). The *Atlas Larmat* recognizes twenty-four 1st *crus*. In addition, Rodier, to accept his lists, including 2nd and 3rd *crus*, mentioned another five. Jacquelin and Poulain bring the total up to forty. But together all these single-vineyard wines come from less than half of this *commune* acreage. All other wine from this *commune*, providing it meets the *AC* requirements, must be sold just as Gevrey-Chambertin. But very fine some of it is. I should say that, over the years, Gevrey-Chambertin represents the best purchase for red *commune* burgundy if you cannot afford single-vineyard wines.

The fault with most *commune* wines sold in Great Britain is, as I have already said, that they are made too heavy. I recall a '57 Nuits-St-Georges, taken at the beginning of '67, when the weather was cold. It was a substantial wine for this *commune*, and quite sweet. Perhaps the shipper, who has a great name, thought that this hard year, full of tannin, needed extra help. Nevertheless, it was not unattractive, at that season. The proof of the burgundy is in the drinking, and the weather affects this. But generally one should only buy red burgundy in which the acids have not been overwhelmed and which is therefore not inert.

You have to take a chance on this in hotels and restaurants, unless you know their wine lists. But in buying for your own table, if you are a good customer, or even only a promising one, your merchant will surely let you taste first. (For the bottle-shopper at the off-licence or supermarket, burgundy, indeed all wine, must always be a gamble.) Or the Londoner can buy at Christie's End of Bin sales, where he can certainly taste first and where excellent *commune* wines can often be acquired at virtually wholesale prices. (At the first of the revived Christie wine sales, in October 1966, *grand cru* burgundies, *domaine*-bottled, sold for about three-quarters of the price of château-bottled 1st *cru* clarets.) The American buyer is protected by the fact that all U.S. importations come in bottles.

Genuine *commune* wines of burgundy are better than *commune* wines of Bordeaux; a Gevrey-Chambertin for example will be better than a St-Julien of an equivalent year. But also a good deal dearer.

Fortunately for the beginner, almost all burgundy is *AC*. We need not bother with the next classification that we find in numerous other fields, the *Vins délimités de Qualité Supérieure* (*VDQS*). This classification includes those wines which rank above *vin ordinaire*, but which are less notable than *AC* wines. They are mainly regional wines and are produced in fairly small quantities. I am told they exist in Burgundy, but I have never come across one, though cynicism suggests that I may occasionally have drunk one in certain hotels, without a *VDQS* label on it.

Finally, to complete the picture, there are certain *vins de consommation courante* that you find in small *estaminets* in Burgundy if you ask for a *coup de rouge* or a *coup de blanc*. But to seek for these seems to be carrying research rather far. It is surely a waste of opportunity, in that country, not to drink something better.

It should be noted in passing that vintages may be mixed within a *commune appellation*, provided that this is stated on the label. For example, you may see a Meursault dated 1962/64.

This is legitimate, and may yield a better wine than the separate years, but I think it will be a less interesting wine.

Numerous burgundy shippers produce branded burgundies. A few of these, such as Latour's Corton-Grancey or de Moucheron's Château de Meursault, are very fine. Geisweiler's Grand Vin, both red and white, has many admirers. In general, however, the branded burgundies, though they avoid the ups and downs of the various vintages, seem to me to be rather dull. I prefer a decent *commune* wine of any reasonable year. In discriminating between shippers it will generally be found that those who rely most on branded wines are inferior to those who concentrate on *AC* ones.

The minimum alcoholic strengths for *AC* wines on the Côte d'Or are: *grands crus*, 11·5° for red and 12° for white; other single-vineyard wines, red 11°, white 11·5°; *commune* wines, red 10·5°, white 11°. For *bourgogne* it is 10° for red and 10·5° for white. *Bourgogne ordinaire*, 9° for red, 9·5° for white. *Passe-tout-Grains*, 9·5°. *Rosé* must be 10° for *bourgogne*, 9° for *bourgogne ordinaire*. Sparkling red or *rosé* must be 9°, sparkling white 9·5°.

5. Some Optional History

After the unavoidable technicalities of the last chapter, we may now have a little light relief.

When, as a schoolboy, I was occasionally permitted to distract my attention from the classics to a subject so unimportant as European history, I kept coming across a puzzling people called the Burgundians. They had not entered my field of knowledge in Caesar or Tacitus, nor on the other hand could I identify them with any of the modern nations of the Continent.

The Burgundii were in fact of Scandinavian origin, and did not get even as far as the Rhine till the beginning of the fifth century A.D. But there was burgundy in Burgundy long before that, because the cultivation of *vitis vinifera* had spread from Italy to Gaul in the pre-Christian era. Pliny (first century A.D.) records that the nobles of the Gallic tribes settled round Auxerre and Mâcon were already drinking wine as well as beer.

A French archaeologist, X. M. Thevenet, found sherds of wine jars in Burgundy dating from 100 A.D., after which there was a gap in the strata of a century or so. This has been explained by the famous edict of the Emperor Domitian, at the end of the first century, which decreed the destruction of all vines in the Empire outside Italy. This was formerly represented as being a measure of protection for the native Italian wine trade. But what in fact Domitian seems to have done was to decree a 50% reduction of the vineyards in the provinces, a measure, probably intended to improve the quality of the wine, which has frequently been repeated, in greater or lesser degree, in later times. Even so, some claim that this edict affected not *all* the provinces, but only Provincia, *the* province; that is, Provence, whose competition might indeed have been troublesome for the Italian vintners. In any case, there was widespread evasion of this law, and it was repealed in 210 A.D. by the Emperor Probus.

Thevenet suggests that during the time-gap in the sherds wine was made in Burgundy, and that the return of the sherds represents the renewal of importation; in fact, that the absence of wine sherds proves the existence of a native industry. Edward Hyams, in his *Dionysus*, argues that wine was stored in wooden casks in the interim, all traces of which have naturally disappeared, and that this shows the Gauls to have been pioneers of the proper method of storing wine. He is supported by William Younger, who in *Gods, Men and Wine* says that funeral monuments of this period depict casks of wine on merchants' carts. Certainly the wine of Burgundy was known by the third century, as in 311 A.D. the rhetor, Eumenes, of the great nearby Roman city of Autun, spoke of the wine of Beaune as if it had been made for some time.

We hear favourably of the wine of Dijon, at the north of the Côte d'Or, in the testimonial of Bishop Gregory of Tours (*circa* 600 A.D.); and now we can return to the Burgundii of my schoolboy studies, who were establishing themselves across the Saône about this time. Some hundreds of years later they seemed, to my juvenile judgement, to have been stout fellows, for they were usually fighting on the side of England. Further knowledge unfortunately revealed that this was less from Anglophilia than from Francophobia. The Franks, later to become the French, were always trying to absorb the lands of the Burgundii into their own kingdom; and in the course of this continuous warfare the Burgundians were ready to turn anywhere for allies. About 800 A.D., by the way, the Franks must have effected some substantial penetration, for Charlemagne acquired vineyards in Corton; hence

Corton-Charlemagne, one of the greatest white wines. Philip Youngman Carter, in *Drinking Burgundy*, relates that Charlemagne forbade the peasants to tread the grapes with their feet – a quite unnecessary piece of nicety, as the alcohol formed in the fermentation is the best natural antiseptic against bacteria.

My juvenile confusion was justified recently when I read in Freeman, the great historian of the Middle Ages, that 'of all the geographical names Burgundy has changed its meaning the greatest number of times. It was first a kingdom, then a duchy (though the premier duchy of all), next a county (corresponding to the Franche-Comté) and fourth a province of France.' At the time of the French Revolution even the restricted province, shorn of its former glories, was divided into the departments of the Côte d'Or, Saône-et-Loire, Yonne and part of Rhône. Which is what we mean by Burgundy today.

Further difficulties were created in my mind by the habit of the kings, dukes and counts of passing on their Christian names to their heirs and, instead of using numbers (perhaps because these would have clashed with those of the French monarchy), adopting sobriquets, some of them of surprising frankness. I at first thought that Charles the Bald was a misprint for Charles the Bold, until in due course the latter turned up too. Then there was John the Fearless; but, rather to my disappointment, I never came across John the Fearful.

I do not think it necessary to set out all the vicissitudes of these worthies. Their story, even if memorized, would hardly help the reader to place a good Burgundian vineyard or evaluate its vintages. But one should call attention to the fact that they were generous patrons of the Church. As early as the sixth century a king of Burgundy gave land near Dijon, 'with its vines', to the Abbey of St Bénigne. A century later we read of vineyards being given to the Church at Aloxe, Beaune,

Gevrey and Vosne; in the next century at Fixin; in the ninth at Chassagne and Santenay; in the tenth at Savigny; and in the eleventh at Meursault and Pommard.

The greatest monastic contribution to wine came about 1100, when the Cistercians created Clos Vougeot. The wall (hence *clos*, enclosure) was built in 1336; it still stands, though obviously much restored. An abbot of Vougeot is said to have sent some of his wine to the Pope, and to have been rewarded with a cardinal's hat. (This has been given for worse reasons.) The Cistercians were also pioneers of viticulture at Chablis. In 1112 the Bernadine nuns endowed the cultivation of what is now Clos de Tart – an unfortunate name, to our ears, for a conventual property.

The connection between the Church and wine is obvious, because of the needs of the Mass. But the output of the monastic vineyards must have far exceeded sacramental requirements and the monks' own needs. They recognized wine as one of God's greatest gifts, and made it for secular sales, as a means of enriching the abbeys to the greater glory of Him who had created this source of wealth.

Even as early as the thirteenth century qualities were beginning to become established. William Younger mentions a comparison of the output of a *vigneron* of Chassagne-Montrachet with the wines of an abbey at Volnay, and the merits of Clos de Bèze were being weighed against those of Clos Corton.

The lay rulers of Burgundy too, as characters of their period go, were enlightened in such matters and favoured commerce, notably in their most important product, wine. Our friend Philip the Bold (he who ruled against the use of the *gamay*) developed protectionist tendencies also. He forbade the storage in his realms of any wine other than burgundy, to prevent blending (or *cuisine*, as the French now call it); a decree that would have been useful in more recent periods.

For a time Philip the Bold, who had inherited Flanders from

his Flemish wife Margaret, moved his capital from Dijon to Brussels. But through the Middle Ages Dijon never lost its pre-eminence, and the grandeur of its ducal court exceeded that of the kings of France. Menus survive in the archives at Dijon of princely banquets of the Duke's Order of the Golden Fleece. The meals went on through consecutive days and nights. One, after beginning with such appetizers as *pâté* of nightingale, fricassees of frogs and snails, and crayfish in aspic, continues with game marinated in burgundy; and we can be sure that the wine was not used only for cooking.

This was a brilliant period for Beaune also, where the Burgundian *parlement* met every other year and where, in 1443, Nicolas Rolin, chancellor of Philip the Good, compounded for his exactions by building the famous Hôtel Dieu, generally known as the Hospices.

But the fifteenth century was at the same time a difficult period for the Burgundian wine trade. There was a devastating plague in the vineyards, which the great Camille Rodier roundly calls phylloxera. Other authorities ascribe it just to 'beetles'. It was so serious that the *vignerons* not only held a religious procession, but all confessed and even undertook to abstain from swearing, which must have been difficult in the circumstances.

Phylloxera came to Burgundy for certain late in the nineteenth century. It appeared on the Côte d'Or only in the 1880s, ten years after its arrival in Bordeaux, but was no less disastrous. The acreage of Burgundy under vines was reduced by two thirds, but we may console ourselves by reflecting that these were mostly *ordinaire* fields. The Côte d'Or was soon re-established by grafting the noble *cépages* of Burgundy onto American phylloxera-resistant roots; and the holy of holies, Romanée-Conti, was never affected. When its original vines had to be grubbed out, this was on account of age.

But I have got ahead of myself. By the fifteenth century

burgundy had established a significant reputation, though this was largely local. The Flemish connection of the court had early taken its wine to Belgium, where it still enjoys great favour and whither many of the best growths are still shipped. Otherwise its land-locked situation deprived it of the wide distribution enjoyed by wines whose vineyards were adjacent to sea-routes, such as claret and sherry. Chablis, being close to the Yonne, which connects with the Seine, was under less of a handicap than the Côte d'Or and southern Burgundy. It was even permitted by the French to reach Rouen (then still in English ownership) and to be shipped to England in the twelfth century, and it is said to have been appreciated by our King John – if that is anything of a testimonial. Much later our Henry VIII imported it by the same route. It reached Rouen in barges, and there was transhipped onto the little cross-Channel freighters. Meanwhile an itinerant monk of the earlier period of our royal favour is quoted as having called chablis 'a white wine, sometimes golden, which has a bouquet and body, and an exquisite full taste' – a fair description, though he omitted to notice the green glints in it.

In the sixteenth century the Burgundian *parlement* set about correcting some of these geographical disadvantages. Burgundy had by now become a part of France in all but name, but it still enjoyed a considerable degree of self-government, and the *parlement* passed measures to improve roads and construct canals linking the Saône with the Seine and Loire. The ending of the wars with France had produced new wealth, and the *parlement* (after having, naturally, adapted the system of taxation to suit the interest of its own members) used the balance of the revenues to promote the wine trade. But they showed a commendable appreciation of quality, forbade the extension of the old vineyards and ordered the rooting-up of those recently planted.

Taxes on wine existed in the Roman republican era. We first find a Burgundian record of them in 1203. They have always been unpopular, and always – till our decadent modern times – more or less evaded.

Paris had been a good customer of wine from Auxerre even in the Middle Ages, and some of this was probably chablis. Halfway through the fifteenth century some Côte d'Or wine was possibly reaching the French court, for Louis XI praised the 1447 vintage of Volnay, though he may have got to know it when he was embroiled with his father and living with the Burgundian dukes. (I liked the 1947.) Two hundred years later red mâconnais was taken up at Versailles. Pierre Andrieu is the source of the well-known story of the giant *vigneron* Claude Brosse, who was so confident of the merits of his wine that he performed the almost incredible feat of driving some hogsheads of it more than two hundred and fifty miles to the capital, over the almost impassable roads of the period, in an ox-drawn cart. We need not go into all the picturesque details of his hegira, but Brosse's physique attracted the attention of Louis XIV and the courageous merchant was rewarded by a regular trade with Versailles. His enterprise certainly deserved an order.

It should be recalled that, apart from the difficulties of transport, there were local tolls everywhere then to hinder the movement of wine from its own field.

Romanée-St-Vivant was prescribed for Louis XIV, who was suffering from a fistula, by his Burgundian physician Fagon, and the king is one of many who are quoted as having said that the remedy more than compensated for the malady. Someone recently commented that the bedside table of the *grand monarque* should have been called his *table de Nuits*.

I have already spoken of the disastrous setback caused to burgundy by the dispossession of the monasteries; but to do the French Revolutionaries justice it should be said that they did not confiscate the vineyards of the Hospices de Beaune, as the revenues from these were used for lay charities. At this time our Arthur Young described 'Clos de Veaujeu' (Vougeot) as the most famous vineyard in Burgundy, commanding the highest price. (The last monastic cellarer at Vougeot, by the way, was appropriately called Dom Goblet.) Earlier religious troubles expanded the market for burgundy. The Burgundian protestants expelled in 1685 took their taste for the wine to Switzerland and Holland, which have remained important markets for burgundy. The early dynastic affiliations and geographical proximity have, as I have said, always made Belgium a large purchaser of this wine. Indeed Belgium used to boast – at any rate up to the 1939 war – some of the finest cellars of Côte d'Or vintages.

Knowledge of burgundy came late to England, apart from the riverborne Auxerre wine imported from the Middle Ages onwards. In the sixteenth century the improvements in vinting introduced by the dukes of Condé (who were granted the Burgundian duchy by the French crown) caused some interest in the Côte d'Or vintages to be shown here, though on account of the costly land freights these were among the most expensive wines on the British market. At the beginning of the eighteenth century the Earl of Bristol had to pay as much as 6s. a bottle for red burgundy; my tables of conversion for sterling purchasing power do not go as far back as that, but the price was very high in terms of our now depreciated currency. Sir Robert Walpole, a great hunter and consumer of game, was a correspondingly great consumer of burgundy. By the third quarter of the eighteenth century appreciation of the different characteristics of the Côte d'Or vineyards was becoming formulated; Sir Edward Baring differentiated between 'wines *de garde*' such as Chambertin and Nuits, which could be kept five years, and '*primeurs*' such as Chassagne, Pommard and Volnay, which only lasted two.

In the nineteenth century the railways came to carry burgundy swiftly and cheaply to the ports, and it became a wine for all countries, particularly for the United States. Dijon is on the main Paris–Lyon–Mediterranée railway line, and its station buffet, by the way, is probably the second best French station restaurant (after the Gare de l'Est at Paris); which is quite high praise.

6. Some Compulsory Geography

The last chapter you could take or leave, though it may have afforded some appreciation of the antiquity of burgundy and the immemorial experience and craftsmanship of its *vignerons*. But this one is important, because you cannot find your way round a burgundy catalogue or wine-list unless you know the layout of the fields. Reading by those who are not familiar with the country should be interspersed from time to time with glances at the map on page 68; otherwise, despite all my descriptive skill, they may lose their way.

It is true that Burgundy is one of the best-known regions of France, for foreigners as well as Frenchmen, for the routes to the Côte d'Azur, to Switzerland and Italy all traverse it. But not many of those who pass through stop to take more than one meal at one of its many famous restaurants, nor to linger among its ancient monuments. Still less do they explore its prestigious vineyards.

Yet, apart from its wine, Burgundy is a rich museum of history and architecture. There are ancient remains from Roman times, glorious Romanesque and Gothic architecture, fine castles and elegant châteaux. For nature-lovers there is the vast forest of the Morvan. And it is a 'paradise for sportsmen', either with the rod or gun. I know of few countries where leisurely travel is better rewarded – especially for the gastronome.

The vine is cultivated in numerous areas of what formed the old dukedom of Burgundy, but none of the outlying vineyards are of much importance now except those of Chablis, and none but Chablis will require extensive consideration in this book.

There are, as was said in our history chapter, four of the modern *départements* that produce burgundy: Yonne for chablis, the Côte d'Or (obviously) for the wines of the Côte d'Or, Saône-et-Loire for chalonnais and mâconnais, and Rhône for beaujolais. The fields in the first are a tiny dot on a map of any but the largest scale; in the three last-mentioned *départements* they form a long narrow strip – in the north not more than a few hundred yards wide, but bulging to the south. It follows the line of the river Saône but is set a dozen miles or so to the west of it, till you get to Tournus, and often astride *Route Nationale* 74 and, for a short space, *RN* 6.

This strip runs from immediately south of Dijon almost down to Lyon; but the best of this again, the fabled Côte d'Or, rich in minerals and source of the great wines, stops near Chagny on the main road, though it continues a little further to the south-west, beyond Santenay on *RN* 14. The Côte d'Or, a string of little towns and villages whose names have become world-famous, along the *Route des Grands Crus* (off *RN* 74), is itself divided into two sections, the more northerly known as the Côte de Nuits, and the more southerly as the Côte de Beaune, each named after its most important town. The former is the home of the greatest reds, the latter of the greatest whites, though there are exceptions in each *côte*.

But since it will be convenient to deal with the main fields by going from north to south, perhaps I had better first clear away the Côte de Dijon, immediately to the south of that city and before you reach the Côte d'Or. As its title suggests, this once had greater importance than it now can claim; indeed, some contemporary writers reject the name Côte de Dijon, which might suggest comparison with the great *côtes*, and merely refer to it as Dijon Sud. Its dense vineyards, when devastated by the phylloxera, were not worth replanting, in view of the expansion of the city. Its former greatness can be inferred from the huge press at Chenove, said to be the largest ancient one in the world. This was erected by Alix de

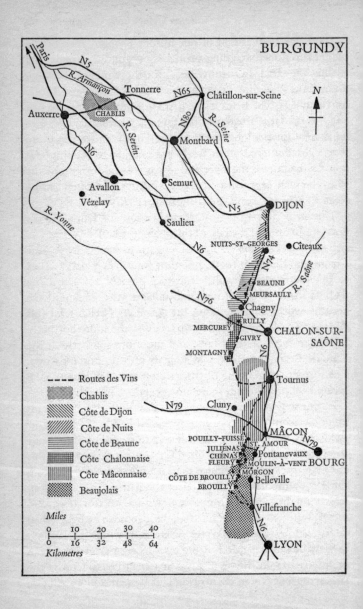

Vergy, widow of Duke Eudes III. Its huge cylindrical block of wood and stone, weighing over twenty tons and moving in a channel fifteen feet deep, is called 'Margot', after Margaret, the wife of Philip the Bold, a somewhat equivocal compliment – but the lady's reputation was equivocal. Chenove, incidentally, is famous also for its snails, one of the principal delights of the Burgundian gourmet. This *côte* produces a light, fresh *rosé* at Marsannay, quite pleasant, if you like *rosé*, for picnic lunches – if you like picnic lunches. There is also *rosé* at Couchey, the next *commune* to the south. In the eighteenth century Marsannay had been known for its reds, but with the growth of Dijon city they turned from the *pinot noir* to the *gamay* for greater yield and its reputation was lost. In the 1920s some 500 acres were restored to the *pinot*, but too late, for the world depression had arrived when they came into production.

The first important vineyards start at Fixin. This, formerly in the Côte de Dijon, is now accepted as being in the Côte de Nuits, though the industrial and suburban spread of Dijon threatens it. On the other hand, only the unimportant *commune* of Brochon (to which further reference is unnecessary) separates it from the great fields of Gevrey-Chambertin.

We are now properly launched into the Côte de Nuits. It ends a little below Nuits-St-Georges, opposite Corgoloin, though Premeaux is its last well-known wine-centre. Here the Côte de Beaune takes over. The southern border of this lies just below Santenay. The Côte de Nuits is about eleven miles long, that of Beaune about fifteen.

Now, still going south, you enter the district known as the Chalonnais, as its heart is roughly opposite the city of Chalon-sur-Saône (not to be confused with Chalons-sur-Marne, the champagne centre). Its important wines are Mercurey, Rully and Givry – the first for its reds, the last two rather for their whites.

Next comes the Mâconnais, west of the city of Mâcon. Much decent ordinary red and white wine is made in the Mâconnais, but the district's distinction comes from the white wines of Pouilly, Fuissé, Chaintré, Solutré and Vergisson now generally lumped together as Pouilly-Fuissé. The best of these are very good, and all the well-made and honestly-labelled bottles are of some quality.

South and slightly west of Mâcon you come to the Beaujolais, the prettiest of these storied Burgundian wine-regions. Its products, long popular in Lyon, later in Paris and then all over France, have leapt into favour in the Anglo-Saxon countries since the end of the Second World War. Perhaps their merits have become somewhat exaggerated, and the demand far exceeds the supply; nevertheless, like the contents of the widow's cruse, 'beaujolais' gushes forth unendingly. The real stuff fills a very useful place in the wine-list for those 'with more taste than money'.

The Beaujolais peters out into the Charollais, superb for beef but inferior for wine, and the Charollais into the Lyonnais, which links the Beaujolais with the Côtes du Rhône without achieving the distinction of either. However, the Lyonnais has a few of the *VDQS* referred to in Chapter 4. But really you need not bother about burgundy south of the Beaujolais proper, which ends a bit below Anse, on *RN* 6.

Before I leave the main line altogether, for more detailed consideration in Chapters 7 to 10, I should mention that each of the three *côtes* to the north (if you accept that the Côte de Dijon is one of these) has a less important bulge to the west, known as the Arrière-Côtes respectively of Dijon, Nuits and Beaune. The last has pretty scenery, particularly round the old fortress of Roche-Pot. These areas have less favourable elevations and exposures than the Côte d'Or, and poorer soil – or perhaps I should say 'even poorer', for all vineyards have poor soil from the horticulturalist's point of view.

In these *arrière-côtes* too many of the vines are *gamay* and *aligoté*, and too few *pinot noir* and *chardonnay*. If one were making a prolonged stay in Burgundy it might be interesting to try some small westerly excursions from the Côtes de Nuits and de Beaune to make comparisons and establish a standard for enjoying the real thing. But I cannot claim any personal knowledge of these wines except that of Arcenant, where I was once delayed by a puncture many years ago and lunched in an *auberge* with some of the local wine, served by the widow of a deceased English jockey of Chantilly. She spoke French with a cockney accent.

Now of the fields separated from the main line the most important, as I have said, is Chablis. Indeed, it is the only important one. It lies between the rivers Yonne and Armançon and is cut by the pretty stream of the Serein. This will be dealt with in Chapter 11. An even more distant field, Les Riceys, is sometimes allotted to Burgundy, because it cultivates *pinots* and *gamays*. But geographically it belongs rather to Champagne, and with a passing word of commendation for its attractive *rosés* I leave it to another volume in this series.

The other detached areas, known as the fields of lower Burgundy – though on the map they are above the Côte d'Or – can be briefly disposed of as far as their wine is concerned, but they are of great touristic interest. The vineyards used to be much more extensive before the phylloxera plague; two thirds of them were never replanted, because only fine fields justified the expense. They must have looked even more extensive, because in those days the vines were planted all higgledy-piggledy, in contrast to the modern neat rows which, it was found, best lent themselves to the new mechanical methods of cultivation. One wonders who drank all their output; certainly in modern times little of it has been shipped, let alone exported. Perhaps however these vineyards account for some of the *bourgogne* one finds in Soho and the supermarkets.

But if you are specially interested in *vins du pays* these may be worth trying as you travel. Therefore the most con-

venient way to cover them seems to be to follow the usual
motor routes to the Côte d'Or, from the Channel coast for
Britons and from Paris for the Americans. The former –
those, that is to say, who have not the sense to go by quieter
if slower roads – go round the west of Paris by the autoroute
to the *A*6, which the latter pick up from the south of the capital. This *A*6 runs down to beyond Avallon, beyond which
those going to the north of the Côte d'Or will fork left onto
RN 70, while those going to its south will continue on *RN* 6
(road indications as of 1968).

Meanwhile however the *amateurs* of local *vins du pays* will
have by-passed some of the scenes of their interests. Perhaps
one can leave out Sens for its wines, though these survive;
however, it has a magnificent cathedral, whose architect did
the Norman parts of Canterbury, and a fine table at the Hôtel
Paris et Poste (M. Sandré). But Joigny, on the old *RN* 6,
has genuine vinous interest for its *vins gris*, paler than the ordinary *rosés*, and Auxerre (the x, by the way, is pronounced ss)
has the best vineyards on this route. These were highly
thought of at the beginning of the nineteenth century, and
the Clos la Chaînette, right against the town walls, is still really
quite good. The town itself *vaut le détour*, as Michelin says, for
its cathedral with fine tapestries. (It was in a street to the south
of this great church that I once saw a meat shop with a fascia
describing it as a *boucherie hippophagique et ânophile* – a nice
distinction.) The nearby Irancy vineyards are fair, though
little red is now made here. It is mostly *rosé*.

In any event you have to turn left near Auxerre if you want
to take in Chablis. And if you have 'done' Chablis and are
going on to Dijon, you would miss some lovely country and
interesting places unless you went to Tonnerre on *RN* 65 and
Montbard by *RN* 5. Both still have vineyards. Besides, Tonnerre has a curious spring, the Fosse Dionne and an old
hospital with good tombs.

This Auxois country, which derives its name from Alesia,

the Gallic fortress that Caesar conquered, is full of ancient fortresses, later habitable châteaux, great abbeys and splendid churches. Any guidebook will locate these felicities for you. They deserve two or three days of a Burgundian tour, unless you are totally dedicated to the wine.

If I have induced the mood for detouring I should recommend another fork off the main road, either to Semur or to Châtillon-sur-Seine – if not to both. Semur has a magnificent situation for its sturdy walls and towers and delicate church. Hereabouts are more romantic castles, elegant châteaux and goodly churches, the last including that of Époisses, home of the famous Burgundian cheese, which also has a curious moated manor house. And there is excellent fishing.

It is not for its wine, though it still makes a little, that I recommend Châtillon-sur-Seine, but for the incomparable *Trésor de Vix*, whose superb Greek artefacts in some mysterious way reached the grave of a young princess of Gallic Burgundy. There is a good restaurant here also, the Hôtel de la Côte d'Or (M. Richard).

If I had to choose a local wine in lower Burgundy (other than Chablis) it would be that of Tonnerre. It was highly praised once by a famous French gastronome, but that too was a hundred and fifty years ago.

And so to the noble city of Dijon, with its splendid restaurants and outstanding Foire Gastronomique held each November. At this you can sample food and drink from all over France – indeed, from all over the world, including Great Britain. (Our Melton Mowbray pies are highly thought of.) There are as many as 400 different cheeses to try! The last time I was there it had a very distinguished visitor, the then papal nuncio in France, who later became Pope John XXIII. In conjunction with it the aforementioned restaurants put on competitive versions of the same menu dictated by the organizers of the fair. These organizers have to test them all, but he would be a very dedicated gourmet among the tourists

who would take the same meal several times over for the sake
of comparing cuisines. The best of these restaurants now, I
think, is at the Hôtel du Chapeau Rouge (M. Mornant). Dijon
is world-famous for its mustard. Grey-Poupon is the leading
vendor, and makes a pretty window-display of this unpromis-
ing material, with his rows of blue and white pots.

The other route, to the south end of the Côte d'Or, now
by-passes the vineyards of Avallon, which lie in the lovely
valleys of the Cure and Cousin. I once tried some of their
wine, not at the famous Poste, which would probably disdain
it, but at an *estaminet* opposite the grand façade of the basilica
of Vézelay. It was at any rate strong. You must go out to see
this basilica, and then you can make your way back to *RN* 6
and make for Saulieu, for the food at the Côte d'Or restaurant,
even though the famous Monsieur Dumaine no longer pre-
sides there. Its menu is too good for Saulieu wine, though you
might try a glass of this as a matter of interest for your aperitif.
Michelin deprived the Côte d'Or restaurant of its three stars
when Dumaine retired, but has restored two of them to his
successor, M. Minot.

From Saulieu *RN* 6 runs through the Arrière-Côte de
Beaune down to Chagny, and so on past the Chalonnais and
the Mâconnais to the Beaujolais. A little before Chagny it
passes through great wine country for the first time, and you
can actually see from it the superlative vineyard of Le Montrachet.

In all of these districts of Lower Burgundy there are still a
number of named vineyards which claim local superiority, but
it seems unnecessary to enumerate them, as they are never
found in wine-lists elsewhere, and if taken locally can be
chosen on local advice.

But talking of names in outer areas, a word of caution
should be added about two minor districts that adjoin the
great one. These are the area called the Plaine de la Saône,
which takes in part of Flagey-Echézeaux (make sure your

Echézeaux comes from the Vosne-Romanée): and the Val de la Saône, which has a Pouilly-sur-Saône that must not be confused with the Pouillys of the Mâconnais.

My advice to the civilized tourist who is not in a great hurry (and civilized people should not be in a hurry) is to keep off the *A*6 and *RN* 6 as much as possible. Every day they are overcrowded with fast, heavy traffic. Then he will be able to lift his eyes from the yellow lines on the road-surface, and take a look at the Burgundian scenery, architecture and vine-yards.

And now, having roughly sketched the secondary and even tertiary wine-areas, we can pass to the heart of the matter, the Côte d'Or – or rather to one valve of the heart, the Côte de Nuits.

7. The Côte de Nuits

After this general survey of the geography of Burgundy it is time to turn to a more detailed account of the principal fields. I begin with the northern section of the Côte d'Or, the Côte de Nuits, and in successive chapters shall work south to the Beaujolais, leaving the outlying field, Chablis, to the last; though by standards of quality it ought to follow the two sections on the Côte d'Or.

The Côte de Nuits yields almost exclusively red wines, from the *pinot noir*, but it has three fine if small white *chardonnay* vineyards. Its reds are usually more full-bodied than those of the Côte de Beaune, take longer to mature, and last correspondingly longer.

This Côte begins with Fixin, and effectively ends with Premeaux, though there are three minor *communes* at the south end that will be briefly referred to at the end of this chapter.

FIXIN. This *commune*, of 105 acres, has a small area of lasting wines of pronounced bouquet. Its best-known 1st *crus* are Clos de La Perrière and Clos du Chapître, both handsome wines. The *commune* wines are good value; they have not enough reputation to be faked, and are usually modestly priced. Outside the village is a pretty public park, with a statue by Rude, who came from here, of 'Napoleon awaking to Immortality' – the sort of work of art that you would expect from its title.

South of Fixin is the minor *commune* of Brochon, which is linked up with those mentioned at the end of the last paragraph but one, and sold as Vins Fins de la Côte de Nuits, or Côte de Nuits-Villages.

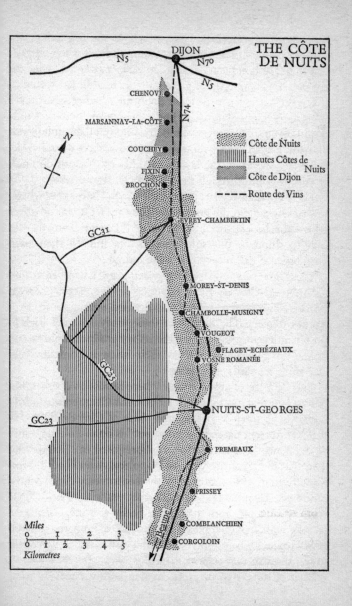

THE CÔTE
DE NUITS

DIJON

N5

N70

N5

CHENOVE

MARSANNAY-LA-CÔTE

COUCHEY

N74

FIXIN

BROCHON

GC31

GEVREY-CHAMBERTIN

MOREY-ST-DENIS

CHAMBOLLE-MUSIGNY

VOUGEOT

FLAGEY-ECHÉZEAUX

VOSNE ROMANÉE

GC25

GC23

NUITS-ST-GEORGES

PREMEAUX

PRISSEY

COMBLANCHIEN

Beaune

CORGOLOIN

Côte de Nuits

Hautes Côtes de
Nuits

Côte de Dijon

— — — Route des Vins

N

Miles
0   1   2   3
0 1 2 3 4 5
Kilometres

GEVREY-CHAMBERTIN. Here, nearly at the beginning, we come on some of the greatest red burgundy. It is the biggest, and fullest of bouquet. These are indeed *vins de garde*, wines to lay down. Chambertin of great vintages used to last for up to fifty years, but it is extremely doubtful whether it will ever achieve such longevity again under present methods of vinification. Even so, Gevrey-Chambertins are still the best burgundies for keeping, and should never be rushed to the table. Generally speaking, the lasting qualities of the reds diminish as you go south through the Côte d'Or from Gevrey.

There are many cellars in the little town. Here, as elsewhere, few *cuveries* adjoin the vineyards. They are set up in the places where the proprietors live. Most of the wine from these is sold to shippers, but some proprietors still do their own bottling, and make very fine wine indeed.

There are two outstanding *grands crus*, Chambertin and Chambertin-Clos de Bèze, covering seventy acres (Clos de Bèze is slightly the larger) and divided among more than twenty owners. The history of these vineyards goes back to the seventh century. Between them they produce about 80,000 bottles in generous years, so their wine is comparatively rare and necessarily expensive.

Clos de Bèze achieved primacy here in medieval times, but I should say that most modern judges rank Chambertin slightly higher. The story is that ancient rivals of Clos de Bèze persuaded a peasant named Bertin to put his small-holding under vines; hence Champ de Bertin, abbreviated to Chambertin. This was the favourite wine of Napoleon, who liked it – this is interesting with reference to the controversy about vinification (see Chapter 14) – at five to six years old. Napoleon, I read, never took more than half a bottle at a meal (generals, teetotal and alcoholic, please note). The ex-Emperor suffered at St Helena by being forced to drink claret, which was easier to transport to that remote island.

Each of these two magnificent wines shows notably what

the French call *une robe* – that is, deep colour – and a full bouquet. They are vigorous, militant wines. There is a much-quoted Burgundian saying about Chambertin, that it is 'like the Good Lord in velvet trousers, gliding down your gullet'. This strikes me as one of the silliest among the many silly sayings about wine. But Chambertin is certainly velvety.

Having condemned the sartorial simile I shall offer one of my own, a musical one. I have often thought that the great *crus* of Gevrey-Chambertin resemble the three big odd-number symphonies of Beethoven. But it is always dangerous to compare the pleasures of one sense with those of another.

There are also six other *grands crus* in this *commune*, Chapelle (12 acres), Charmes (also known as Mazoyères) (78 acres, big for these parts), Griottes (12), Latricières (17½), Mazis (30) and Ruchottes (7½), which are entitled to hyphenate the vineyard name just with Chambertin, and omit the Gevrey, though I do not think anyone considers them quite as good as Chambertin and Clos de Bèze. Indeed, in the *Atlas Larmat* they are coloured yellow; but the *AC* ranks them as *grands crus*. Perhaps they compensate with finesse what they lack in vigour when compared with the two greatest.

There are also twenty-four 1st *crus*, among the best-known of which are Cazetiers, Clos St-Jacques (also known as Village St-Jacques), Combottes, Estournelles and Veroilles. The last (also spelled Varoilles) gains in consistency by being under one ownership. I should never object to being served a bottle of any 1st *cru* here. Gevrey-Chambertin, like Fixin, has two 1st *cru* fields called La Perrière and Clos du Chapître, so it is important not to confuse these wines of the two different *communes*.

On the whole it has been my experience that the Gevrey-Chambertin *commune* wines, from good shippers, outrank the other *commune* wines of the Côte d'Or. It is a biggish area, but the permissible yield in most years (as for Côte d'Or *commune* wines generally) is less than 2000 bottles per acre, so they cannot be cheap. However, they are usually very good.

MOREY-ST-DENIS covers about 325 acres and produces big, sturdy wines, comparable with the Gevrey-Chambertins for slow maturing and long life. They have not acquired as much reputation as they merit.

There are four *grands crus*, Bonnes Mares, though only three acres of this are in Morey-St-Denis and the remaining thirty-three in Chambolle-Musigny, Clos de Tart ($17\frac{1}{2}$ acres), Clos de la Roche (38 acres) and Clos St-Denis (16 acres). The Clos de Tart is under a single owner now, and has consequently improved on its already high reputation. Indeed, at its average price, I should say Jean Mommesin's Clos de Tart is as good a buy as you will find from the Côte d'Or. (There is, too, a splendid old wine-press here.) Count Georges de Vogüé, whom we shall meet again in Chambolle-Musigny, has an outstanding parcel of Bonnes Mares, and makes lovely wine.

Both Clos de Tart and Bonnes Mares were originally conventual vineyards, as the former was founded by a sister-order of the Cistercians, and the latter should really be Bonnes Mères, after the Bernardine nuns who started it.

There are no fewer than twenty-four 1st *crus* here, which shows the quality of the area. The best known is Clos des Lambrays, also under single ownership. It is alternatively called Les Larrets. The others are so little known in the export trade that I shall consign them to the appendix, but one deserves separate mention, because it makes white wine. This is the charmingly-named Monts-Luisants, but it is very hard to find, and the bottle I eventually acquired hardly rewarded the search, apart from being a curiosity. The *Villages* wines of Morey-St-Denis are much appreciated by Burgundian wine men.

CHAMBOLLE-MUSIGNY is a prettier village than most of its rather dull neighbours – dull in appearance, that is – with picturesque galleried houses. Its wine, coming from 450 acres,

is of softer character than those made to its north; in fact it is
the softest of all the Côte de Nuits. It is said to smell of rasp-
berries, as Echézeaux is said to do of truffles and Clos Vougeot
of violets, but I must have an insensitive nose as I never catch
these nuances; good wines of these *communes* just seem to me
to have a lovely vinous bouquet, with Echézeaux the most
pronounced.

The *grand crus* here are Musigny, which goes back to the
twelfth century and whose twenty-five acres are divided
among ten owners, and the remainder of Bonnes Mares, the
larger part (34 acres) of that vineyard. Count Georges de
Voguë makes a wonderful Musigny Vieilles Vignes. There is
also a little Musigny blanc, a fine, full dry wine.

Among the nineteen 1st *crus* of this *commune* Les Amoureuses
is generally accepted as the best. The wine is as delightful as its
name and is appropriately feminine in character. I say 'generally
accepted' because, despite my sentimental feeling for this
field, it must be admitted that Jacquelin and Poulain rate it as
only the top of their 2nd *crus*. Charmes, Cras, Les Combottes
and (subtle distinction) Aux Combottes are other 1st *crus* that
I rate highly.

The *commune* wines are generally good, less full than those
of Gevrey-Chambertin, but still rich. I enjoyed at the beginning of 1967, at the hospitable table of Peter Reynier, a '61
which was so fruity that it seemed rather to belong to southern
Burgundy, but I learned that it had been bottled early, which
perhaps gave it that special character.

There are two of the comparatively rare Burgundy châteaux
at Chambolle-Musigny, neither very old and each called the
Château de Chambolle-Musigny, which is not very helpful.
The older one has splendid cellars.

CLOS VOUGEOT. This is the most famous château of Burgundy, though in fact it is not a château at all, nor for that
matter a monastery (as it is commonly regarded), but the

remains of the *cuverie* and cellars of the Cistercians' lay brothers, started in 1150, with some later sixteenth-century guest-houses for the abbots and distinguished visitors. It will be referred to in more detail in Chapter 12.

The high medieval Clos surrounds 125 acres only, divided among some sixty owners of vineyards at different levels, some indeed on slight reverse slopes, so there is no consistency of quality. The best wines come from the top third of the enclosure (including the rare and lovely Musigny de Clos Vougeot), the next best from the middle third. The wines from the bottom of the slope are unremarkable. Alexis Lichine, in his *Wines of France*, mentions Chioures, Garenne, Grand Maupertuis, Petit Maupertuis, Plante Abbé, Plante Chamel and Quartier de Marci Haut as being outstanding parcels on the higher slopes.

The gesture has been attributed to several generals, even up to the unfortunate Marshal MacMahon, but in fact it seems that it was a certain Revolutionary colonel, one Bisson, who established the tradition, still maintained, that regiments passing Clos Vougeot should halt and present arms. I am all in favour of this military recognition of wine, but personally think the tribute could be better accorded elsewhere on the Côte de Nuits.

The wine of the Clos was sent to the Popes in their exile in Avignon, and Petrarch said that it was this that made them so reluctant to end the schism and return to Rome! One abbot, already mentioned, sent thirty hogsheads to Pope Gregory XI, and four years later – Vougeot, even then, took some time to develop – was made a cardinal.

A property in Clos Vougeot confers an accolade on its owner, and this has caused a kind of *reductio ad absurdum* of fragmentation, because some of the holdings, even of important shippers, do not cover even half an acre. Hence the marked variety of quality already referred to. As an Irishman said, 'You ought to drink your bottle of Clos Vougeot before you buy it.' But the best is very good indeed. I once read a cordial tribute paid to the wines by Stendhal, who was perhaps a more serious judge than Colonel Bisson.

Indeed, in the nineteenth century, Clos Vougeot was ranked with Romanée-Conti and Chambertin and regarded as among the greatest treasures of Burgundy. But this reputation dates from the period prior to 1889, when the Clos was undivided.

The Château de la Tour vineyard, from which the shipper Morin makes a proprietary red wine, cuts into the Clos. Just outside the Clos is a small vineyard called La Vigne Blanche, which makes a very dry white wine called Clos blanc de Vougeot, a 1st *cru*. The vineyard is of less than 5 acres and bottles are correspondingly hard to get, but worth the effort. There are thirty acres of the *commune* of Vougeot outside the Clos, including some good vineyards at Les Cras, La Perrière (here again) and Petits Vougeot. All the rest of the wines of the *commune* are just Vougeot.

FLAGEY-ECHÉZEAUX, with about 150 acres, is mostly on the wrong side of the railroad tracks, or rather of *RN* 74. Its superior fields make a wine resembling both its neighbours, Clos Vougeot and Vosne-Romanée, though perhaps a little harder than the latter. Its *grands crus* and 1st *crus* are now included among those of Vosne-Romanée. Most of the *commune* wines too are sold under the name of Vosne-Romanée – another example of climbing onto the better-known bandwagon. For some reason this is permitted by *AC* rules. So we can pass on.

VOSNE-ROMANÉE. We are now on holy ground. It is here that our Colonel should have given the order to salute if, like a good revolutionary, he had had regard for merit rather than tradition.

The jewels in the crown of this *commune* are small, except for Richebourg, but lustrous. The *grands crus* are Romanée-

Conti (4½ acres), most famous of all; La Romanée, considerably smaller; Richebourg (20 acres); La Tâche, 3½ acres until recently extended to take in Gaudichots which now makes it 15 acres; and Romanée-St-Vivant, 23 acres – plus the two taking their name from the other *commune*, Echézeaux and Grands Echézeaux, of which the former is large, seventy-five acres, and the latter about a third that size.

However, where the vineyards here are small they are divided among fewer owners than usual in Burgundy, so the quality is not only high but even.

Vosne-Romanée was originally the property of the Abbey of St Vivant, but in the time of Louis XV the Prince of Conti acquired it against the competition of Madame de Pompadour, the royal minister against the royal mistress. One feels that he must have had something besides the price of 80,000 *livres* to carry off this contested acquisition. He gave his own name to the best part of the great field, known ever since as Romanée-Conti, the tiny, precious vineyard marked by a cross, which is known as 'the central pearl of the Burgundian necklace'. A church dignitary of Conti's acquaintance, to whom the prince had sent a sample, was the first, but by no means the last, to describe these wines as 'at once velvet and satin'. (No nonsense here about God and trousers.)

Romanée-Conti and La Tâche are now owned by the Domaine de la Romanée-Conti, together with part of Richebourg and Grands Echézeaux, and the Domaine is owned by the de Vilaine family, who are appropriately proud of their possession and care for it accordingly. Of all the tireless weeding operations on the Côte d'Or none is so thorough as that practised here. The buildings of the Domaine are quite modest, but there are splendid cellars; and at the back of the cellars is the 'library' of famous past vintages. M. de Vilaine was the leading pioneer of *domaine*-bottling.

Until 1946 Romanée-Conti retained its pre-phylloxera vines, the proudly named *vignes originelles françaises non reconstituées*.

But the yield was becoming progressively smaller, and the Second World War made their care more and more difficult. They could have gone on for a few more years but for the lack of fertilizers during this period; in the end, however, the roots had to be grubbed up, and new roots were planted and grafted with old grafts. There was no Romanée-Conti between 1945 and 1952.

Romanée-Conti and La Tâche between them only produce about 25,000 bottles in a good year. On account of the small supply, sales are – not unreasonably – conditional; you can only obtain the greatest in a combined order with others. But of course the whole property is very fine.

My knowledge of recent vintages is largely due to the hospitality of the late Guy Prince; their price has been beyond my own purse after the Second War. Each great vintage that I met – the '23s, the '29s, the '37s, the '45s (drunk perhaps too soon) and the '49s (of La Tâche) had some new subtlety; perhaps it is the gilt of distant memory that makes me think the '23s and '29s to have shown the supreme excellence. It was, too, at Prince's fabulous Lebègue tastings, in the candle-lit cellars by London Bridge, that I was able to test, over several years, the new Romanée-Contis after the replanting. They were too young for my amateur judgement to assess, but certainly these stripling wines already seemed better than their contemporaries of other famous Burgundian fields. I do not think it was just the prestige of the names that affected my opinion. In the spring of 1967 I revisited the Domaine and tasted all its '66s. They showed the same precocious magic; there must be some secret of vinification, apart from the merits of the vineyards. We also drank a Romanée-Conti '62, which was already lovely, with the lingering after-taste of a fully-formed wine, though of course it will continue to improve for some time.

Will Romanée-Conti ever be the same as in the time of the old vines? It is a wine slow to mature, and the good years from the new vines are, as I write, only coming to their best. But the soil remains the same, the height and orientation, the care and the pride. M. de Vilaine, by the way, is a great believer in organic manures. The value of the property makes it possible to lavish attention almost on each grape. The present *chef des caves*, M. Noblet, a magnificent type, has responsibility for both the vines and the wines. The management of the Domaine considers these inseparable, but this is only possible on small estates.

Old gentlemen whom I knew when I was younger, who were familiar with the great pre- and post-phylloxera vintages of Bordeaux, were insistent on the superiority of the former. About burgundy I have not found the same consensus. Certainly the old vintages had a lasting quality that their successors have never achieved. The twentieth-century vintages have therefore to be taken younger than their predecessors were. But the general feeling of those best qualified to judge, such as Camille Rodier, seems to be that the finest post-phylloxera burgundies can be ranked with the pre-phylloxera ones for excellence. In any event, it is what is called an academic question. Nineteenth-century vintages, of which rare bottles have survived, have now faded. I am thankful for the great ones of my post-phylloxera lifetime that I have been privileged to enjoy.

Rightly or wrongly I have never ranked La Romanée or Romanée-St-Vivant quite with Romanée-Conti or La Tâche, though as already recounted Romanée-St-Vivant preserved Louis XIV; and in gratitude the town of Nuits has named a street after Fagon, the royal physician, who said of this wine that 'Tonic and generous, it suits, Sire, a robust temperament such as yours.' (Perhaps my own temperament is not sufficiently robust.) But now the Domaine de la Romanée-Conti is managing a large parcel, from the Monge estate, of Romanée-St-Vivant, and it is interesting to see how their care of the vines and methods of vinification give to their Romanée-St-Vivant something of the supreme distinction of

Romanée-Conti and La Tâche. (Their 1966 Romanée-St-Vivant certainly is very promising.)

But Richebourg, which I have bought fairly freely, if not quite so 'supernacular' (Saintsbury's word) as Romanée-Conti and La Tâche is yet good enough for the most exacting taste. It has a wonderfully lingering bouquet, and a superb richness mingled with fascinating undertones of flavour.

These are the greatest red burgundies, with Chambertin and Clos de Bèze their only challengers; but magnificent as these last two are they lack that curious combination of strength and softness that is the keynote of the great Vosne-Romanée wines, which seem like the gentle giants of the legends.

Grands Echézeaux and Echézeaux, as I have said, are included among the *grands crus* of Vosne-Romanée. I personally give a slight preference to the former. It used to be said that these wines were under-priced in England and America because customers were afraid to try to pronounce their names, and so there was little demand. To judge from current price lists, either our French pronunciation has improved or our self-consciousness has diminished. But they are splendid wines, particularly the Domaine's Grands Echézeaux, and worth any price that you can afford.

There are ten 1st *crus* of this *commune*, among which Gaudichots (now incorporated in La Tâche), Malconsorts, Suchots and perhaps Beaux-Monts and Grande-Rue might be considered *grands crus* in other areas. The remaining 1st *crus* (see Appendix B) are all superior wines and can still, as I write, be bought for about £1.25 per bottle as they come onto the market – very little more than the average good burgundy. It is worth looking for these names in your merchant's list. If they are not there, send for a few other catalogues – or perhaps it would be friendlier, in the first instance, to ask your merchant if he could not get some for you.

Vosne-Romanée outside these prestigious vineyards covers about 600 acres in all. Its *commune* wines, including those of

Flagey-Echézeaux that pass under its colours, are in my experience second only to those of Gevrey-Chambertin. They live longer than most *commune* wines and should be given plenty of time to mature. 'It is worse than a crime, it is a blunder' to open them prematurely.

NUITS-ST-GEORGES and PREMEAUX cover about 950 acres. Here we come to the effective end of the Côte de Nuits. Nuits itself is the largest town of the Côte, and the seat of many shippers. It is also the source of much of the sparkling burgundy and Crème de Cassis to be referred to in Chapter 13 – and even of unfermented grape-juice, which seems to have a market. Over Nuits hangs a slightly intoxicating atmosphere, which you can work off by a visit to its fine church of St Symphorien, or even in an excursion to the nearby remains of a Roman town known as Les Bolards, occupied up to the time of the barbarian invasions of the fifth century.

The genuine wines of Nuits-St-Georges are hard to describe. They are dark in colour, through abundance of tannin, but they nevertheless resemble the generally softer wines of the Côte de Beaune. Yet they are not flabby at all; the named vineyards in fact produce a crisp drink, with appreciable bouquet. Even without excessive chaptalization they seem less dry than the more northerly wines; they are, so to speak, dry wines for the sweet tooth.

The outstanding 1st *crus* among the forty officially classified are Les St-Georges (which must not be confused with the *commune* wines of this district), Boudots, Cailles, Cras, Murgers, Porets, Pruliers, Thorey and Vaucrains. These are all very good. A kind and thoughtful man left a number of his friends a small legacy each to be spent on wine, and out of the executor's cheque I personally bought, among other parcels, half a case each of Cailles and Porets '59. I have been drinking them occasionally since the beginning of 1966, and am still keeping one or two; they are not 'over the hill'. They seem a shade delicate for their vintage, but are quite delightful. Porets (also spelled Porrets) is another vineyard owned by a single proprietor.

Unfortunately the *commune* wines of Nuits-St-Georges have been much abused. I am not talking only of the unscrupulous advertisers who have deliberately faked them with non-Burgundian wines. During the famous *Sunday Times* controversy of 1966 it was admitted by certain British merchants that they just used the *commune* name of Nuits-St-Georges for a 'type' wine; they made it of Burgundian elements that would give a result that tasted like what they had decided their customers thought Nuits-St-Georges should taste like. This was really a little too disingenuous. Why subject Nuits-St-Georges particularly to this treatment? Why not do the same for Gevrey-Chambertin or Vosne-Romanée? The matter is, I am assured, belatedly being put right, but for a few years at any rate it would probably be wise, if you want a Nuits-St-Georges, to pay the extra and buy a named vineyard. These are not extravagantly priced.

Premeaux is a small place a little to the south of Nuits. It has a remarkable spring, now transformed into a bathing-pool, which maintains a constant temperature of about 52° Fahrenheit winter and summer. Its wines are allowed by the *AC* rules to be sold as Nuits-St-Georges – at the moment a doubtful boon. Its 1st *crus* are said to be excellent, and since they are not much sought after they are reasonably priced. The one I like best is Clos de la Maréchale, which comes from the largest vineyard on the Côte d'Or owned by a single proprietor; and as its size is only twenty-four acres this demonstrates the exiguity of holdings in general. Of course there are larger vineyards divided between more than one proprietor, and many proprietors own more than twenty-four acres, but not in one vineyard.

The other goodly 1st *crus* of Premeaux that I know are

Corvées (one-man property), Corvées-Paget, Didiers and Forêts.

Beyond Premeaux lie Prissey, Comblanchien (better known for its quarries, which supply some of the finest facing-stone of France) and Corgoloin, whose wines, as previously stated, together with those of Brochon near the north end of the Côte, are generally sold not by their *commune* names, but as Vins Fins de la Côte de Nuits or Côte de Nuits-Villages. They are not bad, but the Côte rather goes out with a whimper.

8. The Côte de Beaune

The Côte de Beaune, some fifteen miles long and generally wider than the Côte de Nuits (though still only a sliver in the breadth of France) takes its name from its principal town, which is full of the houses, cellars and places of business of the wine trade. This Côte embraces 7000 acres as against the 3000 of that of Nuits, but no more acreage of fine red wine, if as much. Indeed, none of its red wine reaches the quality of the finest Côte de Nuits, and only the best growths of Aloxe-Corton and some of the Hospices de Beaune wines can be ranked with the superior northern *crus*. The classified Côte de Beaunes, on the other hand, being more abundant than those of Nuits, often offer good comparative value in the price lists. The reds of the Côte de Beaune are generally softer than those of Nuits, because of a change in the constituents of the soil. They mature more quickly (and therefore should be cheaper), and do not last so long.

In the Côte de Nuits chapter I mentioned a few white wines. These are interesting, but of slight output, and difficult to acquire. The Côte de Beaune, however, produces much superior white wine, and at Montrachet the finest dry white table wine of all.

LADOIX-SERRIGNY is a small *commune* of 338 acres with six 1st growth vineyards which are rarely found in the export trade except for those that have the right to the Aloxe-Corton *appellation*, so we can pass on.

ALOXE-CORTON (the first word pronounced Aloss): Just as the Nuits-St-Georges wines at the south end of the Côte

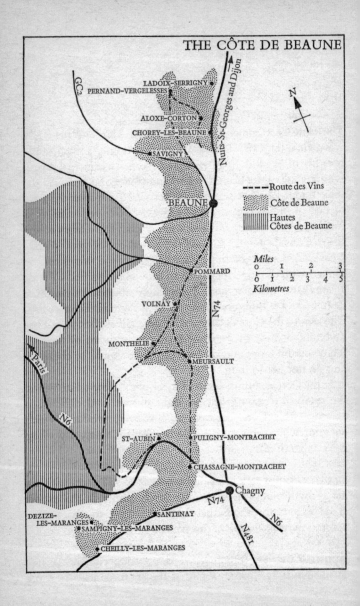

THE CÔTE DE BEAUNE

GC3

LADOIX-SERRIGNY
PERNAND-VERGELESSES

Nuits-St-Georges and Dijon

ALOXE-CORTON
CHOREY-LES-BEAUNE

SAVIGNY

N

BEAUNE

- - - - Route des Vins
Côte de Beaune
Hautes
Côtes de Beaune

POMMARD

Miles
0   1   2   3
0 1 2 3 4 5
Kilometres

VOLNAY

N74

MONTHÉLIE

Paris

MEURSAULT

N6

ST-AUBIN   PULIGNY-MONTRACHET

CHASSAGNE-MONTRACHET

Chagny

N74

N6

DEZIZE-
LES-MARANGES   SANTENAY
SAMPIGNY-LES-MARANGES

N481

CHEILLY-LES-MARANGES

de Nuits most resemble the Côte de Beaune reds, so naturally the Corton reds most resemble those of the Côte de Nuits. This resemblance includes a reluctance to mature and a long life, though the Cortons still come on rather faster than the Gevrey-Chambertins or Morey-St-Denis wines.

The only outstanding *crus* of Aloxe-Corton recognized by Larmat are Le Corton (the *Le* is important here), mostly red, Charlemagne and Corton-Charlemagne (both white). But various vineyards, including Clos du Roi, Bressandes, Chaumes, Renardes, and Pougets have the right to the *appellation* Corton (without the Aloxe-) as certainly 1st *crus*, if not better. Others will be listed in Appendix B. These reds are the best of their Côte, except perhaps for some of the Hospices de Beaune *crus*. They are said to have the bouquet alternatively of violets or blackcurrants.

Red Corton was the favourite wine of Voltaire, and the letter that reveals this preference goes on to tell that while he drank Corton himself he served beaujolais to his guests and household. This has been fixed on by the debunkers to indicate meanness on the part of the philosopher, but anyone who knows about the number of celebrity-hunters and hangers-on that he had to entertain at Verney will applaud his housekeeping. Further, he must have been one of the first persons not a Burgundian to have appreciated the merits of beaujolais.

The whole Corton area belonged for a time to Charlemagne; hence the name of Corton-Charlemagne – the great white wine of this *commune*, and perhaps formerly the second-best white wine of Burgundy. It is said to taste of cinnamon, but here again I cannot follow these nuances – fortunately for me, I should say. To me it has a flinty taste, resembling a fine Chablis but much bigger. Corton-Charlemagne is a large white vineyard, and it is important to buy it from a good proprietor-shipper such as Latour. The ordinary Corton *blanc* seems to me less distinguished but still very good. Wines labelled simply Charlemagne have not been marketed for several years, though Charlemagne remains listed at the head of the *AC appellations*.

Corton Grancey is an excellent proprietary wine of Louis Latour, named after their eighteenth-century château, which has a *cuverie* where some of the pressing is still done by foot. This firm owns about a quarter of the good fields in Aloxe-Corton, and Corton-Grancey is made from the best *crus* and only in good vintages. The bottles are sealed with Domaine seals and the corks stamped with their title and year.

I do not rate the red *commune* wines of Aloxe-Corton as high among *commune* wines as the single-vineyard Cortons rank among the *crus*. Little white Aloxe-Corton *commune* wine is made; it is an acceptable, direct drink, but less subtle than the *commune* wines of Meursault and the areas to the south hyphenated with Montrachet.

PERNAND-VERGELESSES, of 338 acres, is named after the little town of Pernand on the hill behind Corton. It has one outstanding 1st *cru*, L'Ile des Vergelesses, and four others. Its *commune* wines resemble those of Corton, but are said to be harder. However, it is not a well-known area, its prices are reasonable, and a bottling by a good shipper is well worth trying, though there is a difficulty about this since most of these wines are sold under the label of Aloxe-Corton.

BEAUNE, the wine capital of the Côte, is also the most considerable town of the Côte d'Or, with 16,000 inhabitants. It is a big *commune* of 1345 *AC* acres, but less than 200 are of marked quality. The *pinot noir* gives rather soft, light wines here, and there is a fair amount of *gamay*.

Beaune is an ancient town which has, I think, better than most others, preserved the atmosphere of the old French *ville de province*. The boulevards laid round its ramparts, of which a great part remains, carry the 'through' traffic outside the old streets. The Hôtel Dieu, or Hospices, is one of

the outstanding ancient monuments of France, there is a fine
collegiate church which (like the Hôtel Dieu itself) has lovely
tapestries, and the *Logis du Roi*, the one-time quarters of the
Dukes of Burgundy, contains the best wine-museum I know,
and the largest and most remarkable of modern tapestries,
representing 'Wine, source of Life, triumphing over Death',
by Lurçat. There are medieval houses, gates, belfries and
bastions, the last of which contain shippers' cellars, and a number of handsome residences have been built along the lines of
the fortifications. Old convents too contain cellars. There is an
important school of viticulture, and an important oenological
advisory station. Over the whole, on still days, floats a marked
but agreeable odour compounded of wine, wood, mould and
age.

There is an admirable hotel and restaurant, the Poste,
belonging to the Chevillot family – where incidentally (not
that it is of importance to anyone but me) I first met, in 1929,
Siamese cats and a machine for shelling peas. The former have
become more widespread than the latter. I also recommend the
Hôtel et Restaurant du Marché (M. Croix), right in the centre.

The leaders of the twenty-nine 1st *crus* of Beaune are
Bressandes, Clos du Roi (neither to be confused with the same
name in Aloxe-Corton), Clos des Mouches, Cras, Fèves,
Grèves and Marconnets. The finest of the Grèves wines, sold
as Beaune-Grèves de l'Enfant Jesus, belonging to Bouchard
Père & Fils, are quite delicious. They also make a pleasant
proprietary wine, Château de Beaune, made from their
premium vineyards scattered all over the *commune*. Part of
the Clos des Mouches vineyards, owned by Joseph Drouhin,
is planted with *chardonnay* and produces a charming white
wine; but it is not easy to acquire.

The superior growths of the Hospices de Beaune, coming
from 130 acres, not all in the *commune* of Beaune, but all in its
côte, will be dealt with in Chapter 12.

The *commune* wines of Beaune have been much counterfeited and should be bought with care. But, as has already been said, the Côtes de Beaune and Côtes de Beaune-Villages have not generally been considered worth the 'cuisine' treatment, are usually genuine and represent a good choice for comparatively inexpensive table wines. A drive up into the Hautes- or Arrière-Côtes de Beaune is recommended for the scenery.

Erasmus attributed the cure of his nephritis, which he thought to have been brought on by drinking German wines, to his change to Beaune. But it should be remembered, for this and other old references, that 'Beaune' was, up to the nineteenth century, used as a general denomination for red burgundies.

SAVIGNY-LES-BEAUNE (945 acres) is hitched onto Beaune. It has no outstanding vineyards entirely to itself, but shares part of the 1st *cru* Vergelesses with Pernand-Vergelesses and part of Marconnets with Beaune. The Savigny wines, of which a fuller list appears in the appendix, are slightly lighter in colour than those of Beaune, which is the only way I personally can distinguish them, but refined judges say they have less elegance. They offer a nice bouquet.

There is also a small *appellation*, Chorey-Les-Beaune, of 300 acres, whose wines, red and white, I have never come across under that name in England.

POMMARD (850 acres) produces wines light in body but with decent colour, comparatively cheap, popular with the British, but unfortunately not always authentic. (I speak of the *commune* wines. You are protected, of course, if you buy single-vineyard *appellations*.) There are four well-known 1st *crus* among the twenty-six so classified, Epenots, Rugiens-Bas, Rugiens-Haut and Clos de la Commaraine. The last is made at the twelfth-century Château de la Commaraine, a fine building with towers at each corner. The Rugiens wines seem to me to have more body than most Pommards. Contrary to what one would expect, the Bas are generally considered better than the Hauts.

At Pommard the general orientation of the vineyards changes from that of the vineyards to the north. The slopes face closer to the south, instead of to the south-east. It may be this that makes the *commune* wines, even those that are entirely genuine, not very exciting. They are pleasant drinks, but without much authority.

VOLNAY, a hillside town, produces in its 538 acres wine that has been linked with Pommard's by the late H. Warner Allen as a 'twin brother'; but I think Volnay is more interesting, both for the fine named vineyards and the *commune* wines. For one thing, the latter seem in my experience to be less generally 'stretched', though I must still admit to having suffered from some rather peculiar Volnays.

Volnay is less protected by the lie of the land than the other *communes*, and there is much danger of frost hereabouts. If you drive by these fields in the winter you will see the protective heat-pots everywhere ready.

The best-known 1st *crus* of Volnay are Caillerets, Champans, Chevret and Santenots. They are light both in colour and in taste, but agreeable wines with an attractive bouquet. They mature rapidly, so can be enjoyed young, and should therefore be less expensive than Côte de Nuits *crus* of similar rank. Still, the named growths of a good year have a fair life. The Georges Bouchard opened for me in 1967 one of their Santenots '47, a magnificent drink, not at all tired. But it had spent its whole life in one cellar.

Pommard and Volnay have a long history, and some of the old references to them are puzzling till you learn that up to the end of the eighteenth century these wines were what is called *oeil de perdrix*, mixed of 80% red and 20% white.

MONTHÉLIE (233 acres) is only a tiny place, but it has a

separate *appellation*. It has no *grands crus*, but a small number of respectable 1st *crus*. They resemble Volnays in colour, taste and life-span, but are perhaps not quite so good.

AUXEY-DURESSES is another small *appellation* (375 acres), also without a *grand cru*. Its wines are, to my taste, indistinguishable from those of Monthélie, but few are exported and I have had little opportunity of testing them – except for the Hospices de Beaune wine, Cuvée Boillot, which is worth some effort to obtain. Among the 1st *crus* here are Duresses and Bas de Duresses, which a member of the grand council of the *Confrérie des Chevaliers du Tastevin* tells me are noteworthy. Auxey-Duresses also produces some acceptable inexpensive white *commune* wines. Saint-Romain too must be mentioned, as it is a separate *commune*, of 350 acres, but it has no classified vineyards and its output mostly appears as *bourgogne* or *bourgogne grand ordinaire*.

MEURSAULT. Here we come to the predominantly *chardonnay commues*, though red wine is made in some fifty of the 1043 acres. These red vineyards have a different sub-soil. Most of their output is sold as Volnay, as Meursault reds are not commonly known. For example, all the red wine made from the part of the Santenots vineyard that is in Meursault is sold as Volnay-Santenots. The ordinary red wine goes as Côte de Beaune Villages.

Meursault itself is an attractive little town, with a gracious church surmounted by a slender spire, and a Gothic town hall roofed with characteristic coloured Burgundian tiles. Meursault also has its own Hospice, on the model of the larger and more famous one at Beaune. On the outskirts lies the Comte de Moucheron's château, adjoining its splendid, vast Cistercian cellars of the fourteenth century, where over 400 hogsheads can rest. Included is a 'library' of 300,000 different bottles. Here they make the celebrated proprietary wine, Château de

Meursault, from the best *crus* of the *commune*, particularly in Perrières and Charmes. These are château-bottled, with branded corks, quite in the Bordeaux manner.

The great white wines of Meursault rank only after the Montrachet group and Corton-Charlemagne. They are very dry, yet ingratiatingly soft. Some ascribe to them a taste of oatmeal, but I don't eat much oatmeal, fortunately, so am no judge. Others speak of their flavour of peaches, and here for once I am with them, for I can detect this; ripe peaches, almost indeed over-ripe.

The leading 1st *crus* are the aforementioned magnificent Perrières and Charmes. Little if any behind these are Genevrières and the *chardonnay* part of Santenots. However, the Charmes field is divided among too many proprietors, and you should try to buy it from a front-rank shipper. There is also Goutte d'Or, not quite in this rank, but very popular in England and the United States, perhaps because of its name. I am also attracted by the name of another 1st *cru*, Sous le Dos d'Ane.

The white *commune* Meursaults vary in quality according to the standing of their shippers, but the average is commendably high. They are pretty safe wines to buy, but do not last very long. Six years is certainly enough to give them. But the fine *cuvées* are more durable. I split a bottle of Perrières '59 with a *copain* in the spring of 1967, and it was still in great form.

There is a famous local festivity known as *La Paulée de Meursault* which will be referred to in Chapter 12.

PULIGNY-MONTRACHET's vineyards, some 600 acres in all, are much intermingled with those of Chassagne-Montrachet, but I had better stick to the *commune*-by-*commune* formula adopted in this and the previous chapter. Both t's in Montrachet are silent, by the way.

Puligny is an attractive little place with houses with outdoor staircases, but it lacks deep cellars, owing to the high local water-level. So the keeping of the wine is difficult and much depends on its handling. Here, perhaps even more than anywhere else in Burgundy, it is desirable to pay attention to the reputations of the proprietors. Among the best-known are the Marquis de Laguiche, Baron de Thénard, Bouchard Père & Fils and Calvet, who rightly get even higher prices than the average.

Further, these fine wines of Puligny deserve good cellaring at home when you have bought them. If you cannot provide this you should leave them in the care of your merchant until a few days before you need them.

The vineyards here are walled, and different parcels have separate entrances with stone lintels. A number of the owners share the output of their different parcels and employ an expert manager to care for the vines, and for their output up to the stage of bottling.

The *grand cru* – THE *grand cru* – is Le Montrachet, indisputably the greatest dry white table wine. It is partly in Puligny, partly in the neighbouring *commune* of Chassagne. Its principal owners are the Marquis de Laguiche, Baron Thénard and Bouchard Père & Fils. Its pre-eminence dates at least as far back as the time of Rabelais, who called it 'divine', and Alexandre Dumas was inspired to declare that 'it should be drunk kneeling, with one's head bared'. Personally I drink little wine with my hat on and, with my rheumaticky frame, a kneeling posture would not enhance the pleasure of drinking even Le Montrachet.

I dislike this kind of rodomontade, but the excellence of Le Montrachet does almost drive one to rhapsody. It is a great, round, deep wine with a lovely bouquet, and its fullness contains delicate undertones. The Domaine of Romanée-Conti has bought a small plot in Le Montrachet, so as to have the best of the white as well as the best of the red burgundy. Their '66 vintage, tasted in the autumn of '67, had a most distinctive and alluring aroma and should be ready now.

The other *grand crus* here are Bâtard-Montrachet (30 acres), Bienvenues-Bâtard-Montrachet (6 acres only) and Chevalier-Montrachet (17½ acres). Experts differ in the ranking of these, but I should say most put Bienvenues first, with the plain Bâtard and Chevalier equal in the second position, only inches behind in a photo-finish. Pucelles, despite the charm of its name, is not quite up with the leaders. And is it only this name that makes me think it is a little softer than the others? Cailleret and Combettes are also first-rate 1st *crus*.

Blagny is a sub-division of Puligny-Montrachet, and makes an excellent white wine, Hameau de Blagny. Near this is the *commune* of St-Aubin, making both red and white wine of modest distinction, and including the hamlet of Gamay that gave its name to the grape.

CHASSAGNE-MONTRACHET (870 acres) shares Le Montrachet and Bâtard-Montrachet with its neighbour Puligny, and has a white *grand cru* in Criòts-Bâtard-Montrachet. Cailleret, Morgeot and Ruchottes are the best known white 1st *crus*. These are very fine wines, dry but not hard, with an unmistakable bouquet.

Between its two *communes* the supreme part of Montrachet covers less than 20 acres. The maximum yield is under 20,000 bottles. In an average year about 1500 cases are produced. Naturally the proprietors (having read their Omar Khayam, 'I often wonder what the vintners buy', etc.) keep a good deal of this for themselves and their friends. Perhaps about 7000 to 7500 bottles a year go into general sale, for the whole world. The Chevalier and the various Bâtards do not produce much more, but possibly not quite such a high proportion of these is retained by the owners. This is why these wines are so rarely available, and so expensive now when found. (And why, Alexis Lichine points out, you should never miss an opportunity of drinking them.) Yet to think that once, even after the Second War, in an unfashionable Parisian *brasserie* where I was dining on account of parking difficulties, I came across a bottle of Le Montrachet, of a good year, made too by the Marquis de Laguiche, for less than £1.

I have only one reservation to make about this noble wine. Le Montrachet tends to maderize with age. I was once served a bottle by a proud host which had turned golden, instead of retaining its pale, greeny-straw tint. It was past its memorable best – but how good still.

When you examine the lie of the terrain here and at Puligny you can at once see the reason for the different qualities of the different *crus*. Le Montrachet has an absolutely perfect elevation, orientation and slope. It holds the sun from rise to set. And it commands a price which – as at Romanée-Conti – allows for the most meticulous cultivation.

All of these firm white wines of the Côte d'Or, even *commune* wines included, can be taken not only with fish and cold meats, but with hot lamb, chicken and even beef. They will stand up to anything except game and strong sauces.

Chassagne-Montrachet also has four excellent red vineyards, Boudriotte, Clos de la Boudriotte, Clos St-Jean and Morgeot. These and a few others are ranked as 1st *crus*. In any event, in a good year these are finer wines than is generally recognized. They are, therefore, for their quality, comparatively inexpensive, and often represent better value than the top *crus* of *communes* more famous for their red wines. Also they come on quickly, which is another factor making for economy in their purchase. Clos St-Jean seems a bigger wine than the others, and has some of that natural, unchaptalized sweetness that is often mistakenly accepted as characteristic of red burgundy in general.

Both white and red *commune* Chassagne-Montrachets are very good in a good year. They served a red '59 at a dinner of The Wine & Food Society in November 1966 which I thought was first-rate. It seemed at first a modest wine, but it had plenty of *panache* as it developed in the glass, and went admirably with quail. But one would have wanted something bigger for higher game.

Cheilly, Dezize, and Sampigny-les-Maranges are minor *communes* making both red and white wines, with a few 1st *crus*, but the effective end of the Côte de Beaune, and so of the Côte d'Or, is:

SANTENAY, large (950 acres) but not an important *commune*, yet providing a sympathetic little coda to the symphony of fine burgundy. It has no *grands crus* and only three 1st *crus*, of which Gravières is the best known. Most of the wine is red. It is undistinguished but attractive – the sort of drink that you call 'a nice wine', providing a bridge between those of Chassagne-Montrachet and of the Côte Chalonnaise. The *commune* wines are enjoyable, comparatively inexpensive, and usually quite genuine. There are also a few white Santenays, which have a markedly high alcoholic content.

The village of Santenay has a thermal station, with even a casino if you want to chance your luck at the end of this golden road. The waters are said to be the most highly lithinated in Europe, whatever that may import.

9. The Chalonnais and the Mâconnais

The Côte Chalonnaise is the smallest and least important of the fields of southern Burgundy, and makes only some 1,800,000 bottles a year, of which less than a quarter is white. It begins south of Chagny and ends north-west of Tournus, where the tourist who is not entirely absorbed in oenology should inspect the fine basilica of St Philibert.

The Côte is named after the city of Chalon-sur-Saône, where incidentally I experienced, in 1947, the hottest night I have ever known in Europe; a night passed mostly in the hotel bath, which ran warm water even from the cold tap – and this, for once, not through a misconnection in the plumbing. This hotel, the Royal, had a good restaurant when I was last there, and I know of no reason why this should not still be so.

But Chalon is not an interesting town, and the wines made in the plain round it are not interesting either. However, as the vines climb the foothills the product improves, and Mercurey, Givry and Rully are quite reputable names. Their bottlings should be markedly less expensive than those of the Côte d'Or; otherwise they would not be worth importing – though they are pleasant for local drinking.

Mercurey is the most famous. It is named after a former Roman temple to the messenger god, now replaced somewhat prosaically by a windmill. It has ten 1st *crus* which are required to reach 11° alcohol for the red. They are Barraults, Byots, Champmartins, Crets, Clos l'Evêque, Nogues, Tonnerre, Vignes Blanches and Grands and Petits Voyens. These can be sold under their names or just as Mercurey 1st *cru*; unnamed vineyards need only give 10·5. The few whites require half a degree more in either case. The red wine is soft in body, like the less important wines of the Côte de Beaune, but it is darker in colour and has a pronounced taste that you can soon learn to distinguish. It also has some bouquet, and good years are worth keeping to give time for development. Some *vin rosé* is also made here.

Givry red is dark like Mercurey, more robust in taste, but lacking in subtlety; an acceptable wine, but obvious. It has a number of named vineyards, including Barande, Bois Chevaux, Cellier aux Mornes, Champ Nallot, Clos St-Paul, Clos St-Pierre, Clos Salamon (very biblical, these), Marolles and Survoisine. There are also superior growths in the nearby district of Touches, which once enjoyed a high reputation.

Rully reds also have more body than those of Mercurey, and they are good lasters. The 1st *crus* may be sold under that classification, prefixed by 'Rully', or may quote their vineyard names, Cloux, La Fosse, Marisson, Mont-Palais, etc. But I consider Rully more important for white wine. It has white 1st *crus* that are worth looking out for – including Grésigny (which I have met in London), Margotey, Raboursay and Raclot. These wines have an appreciable bouquet and some delicacy of taste. Some sparkling white burgundy is made here.

The percentages of alcohol required for Givry and Rully are the same as for Mercurey, and in all the superior vineyards the grapes used are the *pinot noir* and *chardonnay*, though the AC rules permit the use of the related *beurot* and *liebault* for the red.

Montagny (in full, Montagny-les-Buxy) is not up to these, but it is better than the Chalonnais *ordinaires*. Its whites are really quite acceptable. Much of its red wine is turned into sparkling burgundy, which shows that the proprietors do not think much of it.

The ordinary run of the unnamed Chalonnais vineyards is planted with high-yielding grapes, *gamay* and *aligoté*, though the *gamay* does not do nearly as well here as in the Beaujolais.

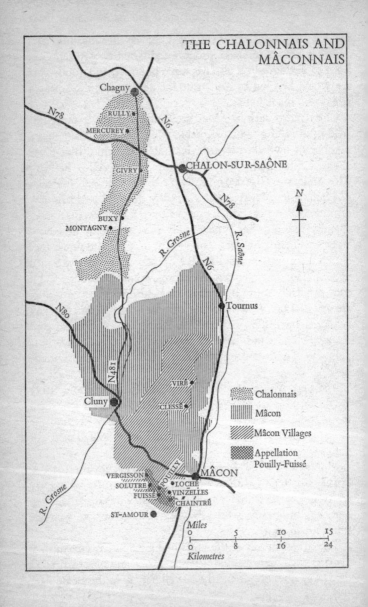

THE CHALONNAIS AND
MÂCONNAIS

N78

Chagny

N6

RULLY

MERCUREY

GIVRY

CHALON-SUR-SAÔNE

N78

R. Saône

N

BUXY

MONTAGNY

R. Grosne

N6

N80

Tournus

N481

VIRÉ

Cluny

CLESSÉ

⬛⬛ Chalonnais

▨▨ Mâcon

▧▧ Mâcon Villages

▩▩ Appellation
Pouilly-Fuissé

MÂCON

VERGISSON
SOLUTRE
FUISSÉ

POUILLY

LOCHÉ
VINZELLES
CHAINTRÉ

ST-AMOUR

R. Grosne

Miles
0   5   10   15

0   8   16   24
Kilometres

You may have tasted some without knowing it, as the northernmost vineyards are entitled to the *appellation* of Côte de Beaune Villages. Most of the rest that is exported goes as *bourgogne ordinaire*. They all can be drunk young – and should be.

It is probably unnecessary to add – but I am very conscientious – that Château Chalon has nothing to do with the Chalonnais. It is the finest *vin jaune* of the Jura, a curious golden wine somewhat resembling sherry.

My happiest recollection of Mâcon is of the Hôtel de l'Europe between the wars, where Burtin, the repatriated chef of the Kaiserhof Hotel in Berlin, set such a wonderful table. And though he offered all the great wines of the Côte d'Or, the one he recommended was Pouilly-Fuissé, not so well known then as now, nor ranked so highly as it is today. The void in Mâcon left by Burtin's death has been filled by the admirable Auberge Bressane (M. Duret).

Before we get to Pouilly-Fuissé and the other wines of the Mâconnais, let me mention for those interested in such things the Rocher de Solutré, in the Pouilly district, which is a striking formation from which many exciting prehistoric finds have been excavated. In the village there is a tasting cellar, the Caveau de Pouilly-Fuissé.

The Côte Mâconnaise begins about opposite Tournus where you can eat well at the Restaurant Greuze (M. Ducloux), and runs down below the city of Mâcon to the west of RN 6 and astride RN 481 to about Romanèche-Thorins, where there is another Hospice with a foundation similar to that of Beaune. Its wines are sold as Moulin-à-Vent des Hospices de Romanèche-Thorins. There is a sign-posted *Route du Vin* on RN 481 and the Mâconnais fields begin near Cormatin, where there is a pleasant château. Near the Pouilly district, in the south of the area, lies the Domaine de Beauregard, with a wonderful view. Then working back to RN 6 just north of Mâcon you find the Maison de Vins du Mâconnais, where one can in-expensively taste all the wines of the Côte.

But before becoming totally absorbed in these you should not miss detouring west from the *Route du Vin* to the abbey of Cluny. The present remains are meagre, but in its heyday it was the largest in Christendom, and with the other famous abbey of Cîteaux it played the leading part in the Burgundian development of viticulture, and out of mere piety no wine-pilgrim should miss it. This piety may be rewarded by an excellent meal at the Restaurant Moderne (M. Chanuet). Permission should also be sought to visit the National Stud with (gratifyingly) its English thoroughbred stallions.

For some reason the Mâconnais is less subject to cold winds than the Côte d'Or, and its summers tend to be hotter. Generally speaking, the south-facing vineyards here produce the best wines, but in very hot years (e.g. the aforementioned '47, and in '59) the normally less-favoured vineyards with other aspects do better. The point of this remark is that in off years mâcons offer better value than the small wines of the Côte d'Or.

The whole Côte Mâconnaise has an annual average produc-tion of 2,000,000 cases of wine, of which at least half is red. But it is the whites that are better known in Great Britain and the United States, and of these whites the most famous are the Pouilly-Fuissés, of which one can hope for 200,000 cases odd, plus 16,500 of Pouilly-Vinzelles and 5500 of Pouilly-Loché.

Chaintré, Fuissé, Pouilly, Solutré and Vergisson are the villages that are entitled to the important Pouilly-Fuissé *appellation*. Single-vineyard bottlings (such as Berthelots, Boutières and Vignes Blanches) are superior, and worth seeking out. The Château de Fuissé is a proprietary 1st *cru* of M. Vincent, reliable because it is only sold under that label in good years. Another proprietary, Château de Pouilly, shipped by Mommesin, is well known. Again I risk the obvious by remarking on the distinction between Pouilly-Fuissé and Pouilly Fumé (made of the *sauvignon* grape, there called *blanc fumé*) on the upper Loire.

Pouilly-Loché and Pouilly-Vinzelles are separate *appellations*, only slightly inferior to Pouilly-Fuissé. Named vineyards should reach 12° alcohol, others 11°. For all of these better wines, including the generic mâcon *blanc supérieur*, the *chardonnay* should be used. If the *aligoté* is used the bottle must, in France, be labelled *bourgogne aligoté*, but *bourgogne grand ordinaire* and *bourgogne ordinaire* are permissible labels for export. Unfortunately, with British bottling information about the grape is rarely given, and this all-important matter is left to the consumer's palate.

The Pouilly and other good white mâcons have a greenish tint in their gold. They give off an appreciable bouquet which is said to be reminiscent of hazel nuts, and the taste is compared with gun-flint. They are heady in youth, when they also tend towards excess acidity, though they come on quite quickly, and are generally not long-lived. The ordinary mâcon *blanc* can be enjoyed at three years, but a good one will not be at its best till five, and I have known them to exceed this span.

I say 'a good one'. They are good wines, rather than great, generally, even the best of the Pouilly-Fuissés; but they sometimes rise above themselves. I came across a bottle of '59, at Coventry of all places, that struck me as being remarkable. Having traced it back to the importers, Grants of St James's, I ordered a few cases and a month or so later served a couple of bottles at the beginning of a little dinner at which a celebrated wine-buyer was present. He spotted the year all right, but thought that it was a Meursault, because of the peach-like flavour.

There are white mâcons sold with the *commune* names of Clessé, Chardonnay (said to be the birthplace of the grape), Lugny and Viré, and some add their vineyard names as well. These are quite good.

However, now that beaujolais has become so famous and popular, a number of the bottlers took to selling their mâcon *blanc* as beaujolais *blanc*. In some areas, to the south of the Mâconnais, there was an *AC* choice of *appellation*; but too often the naming is just a matter of the shipper's judgement of public fancy. The reader will probably have noticed the marked increase in the supply of beaujolais *blanc* in recent years. In any event, whether mâcons or beaujolais, these *ordinaires*, and still more the *supérieurs*, are attractive little wines, very satisfactory if you have a thirst. They are not worth laying down, but it is nice always to have a few.

The white mâconnais go well with fish and cold meat, and the Pouillys are excellent with that wide classification of *pâtés*, *terrines* and sausages that the French know as *charcuterie*.

Now there is a new *appellation*, St-Véran, to which wines coming from a number of villages round Pouilly-Fuissé are entitled. These are wines that might hitherto have been sold as white mâconnais or white beaujolais. Theoretically these should now all be classified as St-Véran; but some shippers are permitted to retain the title of beaujolais *blanc*.

No mâcon *rouge* achieves as a red the quality of a Pouilly-Fuissé as a white; but the red can be a very agreeable wine, though it is rough in youth. It is fuller-bodied than beaujolais, but perhaps harsher. It is wise to pay a shilling or so more per bottle for a mâcon *supérieur*, and even a bit more for named bottles such as Azé, Charnay, Creuses Noires, Davayé, Lugny, St-Véran, Sennecey, Sologny and Verzé. There is also an *appellation* of Mâcon Villages, with the same restriction as to grapes and alcoholic strength as for mâcon *supérieur*, but coming from specified areas of modest merit.

Some red mâcons are made from the *pinot noir* and the related *beurot* and *liebault*, but these do not do so well here as on the Côte d'Or, and the best red mâcon comes from the *gamay noir à jus blanc*, though the *gamay noir à jus coloré* (or *gamay teinturier*) is tolerated (in the Mâconnais, but not in the Beaujolais) up to a maximum of 15%.

There is said to be a trick in some of the mâcon *rouge* districts of mixing up to 15% white grapes with the red during the vinification to give the wine a brighter appearance; but I do not know how you can find out about this. Here again, as always, your safeguard is your merchant; measure him well. But it is quite legitimate, in poorer areas where the *gamay* makes too rough a red, for the *vignerons* to turn over to *rosé*. I am not a great lover of *rosé*, but these Mâconnais ones are fresh and enjoyable. Some reach 10° alcohol, but most are about the innocent 9°.

The best red mâcons used to be made round Romanèche-Thorins, but again with the sensational rise in the repute of beaujolais these have climbed on board the fashionable band-wagon and are calling themselves Moulin-à-Vent. St-Amour, like Moulin-à-Vent a classified beaujolais growth, is geographically in the Mâconnais, because the real border between these areas is that between the *départements* of Saône-et-Loire and Rhône. These transmutations are authorized, but I am afraid that there are many mâcon bottlings following the new fashion (at any rate in British lists) without the same justification of having been grown on the granitic soil, found at the south of the Mâconnais too, that is typical of the Beaujolais.

It would be a pity to let mâcon *rouge* disappear altogether, because it is a sturdy, honest wine, unlikely to be faked, and markedly different, in most cases, from the true beaujolais with which it is now being confused.

10. The Beaujolais

Youngman Carter roundly declares that beaujolais is the best of all cheap red wines, and I should not till recently have quarrelled with the statement. It is made from a generous grape, with a high yield per acre. It matures quickly, so it is not loaded with bankers' charges. It ought to be inexpensive, but particularly with the outstanding *cuvées* it is no longer so.

It is alternatively called a 'quaffing' or 'gulping' wine. You want to take great draughts of it – not too great, I hope, at lunch when motoring, as it can be heady stuff when young and has been known to run up even to 15° alcohol on favoured sites in great years. It is the only red wine that really quenches thirst.

And there is an engaging simplicity about it. Though its merits differ widely, and are worth noting, it is never a complicated wine that you have to analyse reflectively. It is a friendly and unsophisticated drink which can be used as an aperitif, a table wine, or even as a nightcap. A friend of mine who is a leading buyer and merchant tells me that when he is alone for dinner – after tasting all morning, and perhaps taking three or four great vintages at lunch – he always drinks beaujolais. It relaxes his concentration.

Though the sale of white beaujolais increased, particularly when so many Mâconnais wines were being bottled under that label, the great mass of beaujolais is red, and it is to be understood that in this chapter, until near the end, I am talking of the red.

Beaujolais was almost unknown in Great Britain and the United States until after the Second World War; indeed, it was hardly known in France outside its own region, Lyon and a few Parisian bistros before the First War – though Voltaire, as I have recorded, appreciated its merits over two hundred years ago. I must confess that I twice drove through the Beaujolais in the 'twenties without paying any special attention to it, thinking that the real burgundy fields ended, if not at Santenay, at any rate at Pouilly. France was continuously devaluing its currency in those days, living was cheap for visitors with sterling, and in the great Lyon restaurants I drank, not a small beaujolais from a carafe, but fine vintages of the Côte d'Or.

Now beaujolais is the most popular wine in France, and almost equally so in export markets. Imports into Great Britain were trebled between 1964 and 1966; demand increased even more – with the inevitable result. Much of it is stretched with wines from the Midi and even North Africa; some, I fear, of what you see in cut-price shops is not even stretched, but entirely unauthentic. So the inevitable, boring caution has to be repeated. Never buy an ordinary beaujolais unless you have tasted it or a trustworthy merchant has vouched for it; it is usually worth paying a bit more for the named *commune* growths. Among a number of reliable shippers mentioned in Appendix G, I have always found Thorin and Duboeuf most satisfactory.

The nine named *communes*, in the order of the price they generally fetch, are, starting from the top: Moulin-à-Vent (under which *appellation* the Romanèche-Thorins wines are now mostly sold, but if these appear under their own names they should be good), Côte de Brouilly, Juliénas, Fleurie, Brouilly, Morgon, Chénas, St-Amour and Chiroubles. Chénas sometimes climbs higher in the price-list, and St-Amour can also rise above its ordinary valuation. These wines should all give at least 10° alcohol, and Côte de Brouilly 10·5. In all of these districts there are named vineyards, such as Brouilly Château de Briante, which should give you outstanding little wines – or perhaps even something better with

11°. Americans are particularly keen on this single-vineyard bottling.

It may be helpful, as a guide to buying, and particularly to keeping, if I try to sum up the various characteristics of these leaders of the Beaujolais. Naturally the different fields vary from year to year – though there is not usually as much difference between vintages here as on the Côte d'Or:—

Moulin-à-Vent (1750 acres), a dark, full wine, takes longer to mature than its neighbours. It should be left till it is five years old, and in good years will last correspondingly. I kept a '49 Moulin-à-Vent till 1961; it had lost colour and appeared to be almost an 'onion skin', but was still very good, certainly the equal of some well-known lesser growths of the Côte d'Or at a similar age. But this was exceptional longevity.

Côte de Brouilly (500 acres), lighter in colour but rich in taste, reaches its peak in three or four years; it should not be kept much longer.

Juliénas (1325 acres), a medium stayer, is sometimes rather harsh in youth except in good years.

Fleurie (1750 acres) is light in colour and body, a silky wine, to which a French authority attributes the quality of 'plumpness', whatever that may be. It is nearly always pleasant, and very popular in the United States. It matures quickly, and normally should be used up by its fourth or fifth year.

Brouilly (2000 acres), similar but slightly inferior to Côte de Brouilly, should be taken earlier, say in two to three years.

Morgon (1375 acres) is full-bodied, but not coarse; it develops quickly.

Chénas (450 acres), though a little hard, matures early and only lasts well in fine years.

St-Amour (538 acres) is rich in colour but light in taste; it needs some age, but not much.

Chiroubles (625 acres) makes robust wines of distinctive flavour. These are quick starters and medium stayers.

All of the preceding remarks on the drinking and keeping of these wines ignore the taste for the beaujolais *de l'année*, which will be discussed later. But surely no one would exercise this taste with Moulin-à-Vent.

Between and round these superior fields are those of Beaujolais Villages, the next best grade covering about 4250 acres. Sometimes the name of a village, other than one of the nine aforementioned, is attached to the wine; thus, Beaujolais-Odenas. This too must run to 10° alcohol, as does beaujolais *supérieur*, the third grade. Finally comes beaujolais (9°). Between them these cover about 23,000 acres. Much of this last is no longer made by the smaller proprietors, but by the co-operative wineries, to which they sell their grapes. About 30% of beaujolais is co-operative-made, but only about 10% co-operative-bottled, mostly sold to the United States as a form of 'estate bottling'. The balance is either bottled by shippers or sold in the wood for the carafe trade. Very decent some of this last can be, in its simple way, if the restaurant-owner knows how to buy and takes a pride in his drinks. When the co-operatives bottle beaujolais they often do so in the convenient-sized *pot*, two-thirds of the size of a standard bottle.

As I said in Chapter 4, good beaujolais is made from the *gamay noir à jus blanc*, which gives it its rich colour, fruity perfume and refreshing acidity. This grape thrives on granitic soil and seems to shed there all the metallic tang that makes it a second-rater on the Côte d'Or. On the other hand the *pinot noir*, pride of the Côte d'Or, does not succeed in the Beaujolais. It is permitted, with its variants of *beurot* and *liebault*, in ordinary beaujolais but excluded from named growths.

The *gamay noir à jus coloré*, tolerated in the Mâconnais, is now forbidden in the Beaujolais. It gives an artificially deep colouring, its taste is coarse and iron-like. Good beaujolais should have body, but its predominant taste is fruity, not mineral. It is a fragrant wine, always reminiscent of the grape itself – like grape-juice, in fact, but with the added interest, and effect, of fermentation.

Indeed, so distinctive is this wine, in its representative form, that it is questionable whether it should ever have been classified as burgundy. It is made from different grapes, on different soil. It is big enough, with its average annual output of 6,500,000 to 7,500,000 cases,* to stand on its own merits, which are considerable. Bordeaux too is a wide classification, but after all Blayais or Côtes de Fronsac basically resemble a médoc in all but finesse; but there is no similarity between a beaujolais and a Côte de Nuits, and little between it and a Côte de Beaune. However, rightly or wrongly, the decision has been made. Beaujolais is burgundy.

There are two other disputable questions about this wine; at what age, and at what temperature, should it be drunk?

It was Jules Romains, of the Académie Française, who first told me about the beaujolais *de l'année*, the yearling wine, also known as beaujolais *nouveau* or *primeur*. He used to make an annual pilgrimage to enjoy it from *pichets*, in the manner of the Beaujolais folk themselves, when the *vin de primeur* is quite new, richly dark, and still a little *pétillant* from its recency of fermentation. This habit has spread throughout France, and has lately been promoted in England. It is legitimate to put this on sale by 15 November following the vintage.

Now it is true that most beaujolais – not, I repeat, Moulin-à-Vent or the other big growths – is mature in a year, and that four years is the natural life-span of these wines that come on so fast. Unfortunately most of the beaujolais sold in Great Britain, and certainly some that I have had in the United States, is excessively loaded for the supposed taste of foreigners; and such wines are certainly not agreeable in the first year. If you want to follow French fashion out of France you must make sure that your supplier has imported a natural wine.

* How many cases are *sold* as beaujolais each year? This figure is not available.

Then the beaujolais *de l'année* is like an amusing impromptu, in comparison with the studied work of art represented by a *vin de garde*. In any event, all beaujolais, whenever it is to be consumed, should be bottled early.

It may seem paradoxical to take a beaujolais *de l'année* in magnums, but J. B. Reynier Ltd put up some Fleurie '66 in that style, and in July 1967 it was magnificent of its kind. Perhaps a wine that you are going to gulp gains by being bottled in large containers, just as much as a distinguished *cuvée* that you are going to sip.

In a poor year like 1965, when the wine shows little promise of maturing well, it is best to sell and drink it all as beaujolais *de l'année*. Even in a good year you may have different styles; the lighter *cuvées* are then given a brief fermentation, bottled quickly and sold to be drunk soon. But some of the fuller, darker wines, given longer fermentation, will mature slowly and last the ordinary life of this wine.

Then there has been the discovery of the Beaujolais habit of drinking beaujolais, if not chilled, then certainly cool, straight from the cellar. But we in England, regarding it as a red wine, have in the past given it the usual treatment of chambering. Which is right?

A few years ago an enterprising London merchant gave a tasting for the wine-journalists of a number of different marks of beaujolais, with one bottle of each chambered and the other brought in straight from the cellar. Perhaps (if I am not too cynical) it was because the idea of cool beaujolais had just begun to circulate that the majority voted for the cool versions. But I begged to differ. It was a characteristic London summer day, cold and wet, and most of the selections were of the finer growths. I thought, in these circumstances, the bottles that had been chambered afforded the greater pleasure.

As so often in matters of food and drink, climate is a decisive factor. When you are in the Beaujolais you are already quite far south. A cool bottle of a young little growth, brought

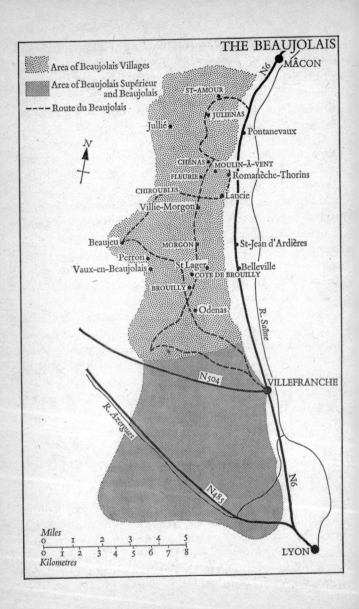

THE BEAUJOLAIS

MÂCON

Area of Beaujolais Villages

Area of Beaujolais Supérieur
and Beaujolais

Route du Beaujolais

ST-AMOUR

JULIENAS

Jullié

Pontanevaux

CHÉNAS

MOULIN-À-VENT

FLEURIE

Romanèche-Thorins

CHIROUBLES

Lancie

Villie-Morgon

Beaujeu

MORGON

St-Jean d'Ardières

Perron

Vaux-en-Beaujolais

St Lager

Belleville

CÔTE DE BROUILLY

BROUILLY

Odenas

N504

VILLEFRANCHE

R. Azergues

R. Saône

N6

N485

N6

LYON

Miles
0   1   2   3   4   5
0 1 2 3 4 5 6 7 8
Kilometres

on a sunny day straight from the cellar, is delicious. In our north I think the more important wines, at any rate, gain by chambering for a few hours and even by decanting – certainly by being allowed to breathe for an hour. In the United States, where room-temperature (naturally or artificially) is so much higher than in Great Britain, beaujolais certainly does not need chambering, though it helps to give it a few minutes to breathe after the cork has been removed. On the other hand, in some American air-conditioned restaurants, it really needs a little coddling of the glass in the hand to bring out its fruitiness.

I think a sensible compromise would be to say that beaujolais takes to chilling better than any other red wine, if you want a long, thirst-quenching draught; and that it is a sturdy, care-free wine anyhow, so that if you have lacked the forethought, at home, to chamber it, you can take it straight from the cellar or cupboard and lose little if any of the enjoyment.

The Beaujolais country is more rolling and wooded than most of the Burgundy fields, and is an engaging area for a few days' motoring. From its higher hills you can see to the Jura and the foothills of the Alps. From the church on the top of Mont Brouilly the view even reaches, on clear days, to Mont Blanc. If you want to go there for the vintage you should count on it being earlier than on the Côte d'Or – soon after the middle of September.

The villages have a sunny allure in summer, and the white cottages and little chapels among the vineyards are delightful. But the autumns often experience devastating hail (1966 was an example) and the springs are full of hazard; oil-stoves are then always ready to be lit among the vines, and a nightly vigil is kept if the thermometer nears freezing-point. In May 1967, despite precautions, the loss from frost was considerable.

The people here seem to have the frank charm that marks their wine, though when you come to purchasing you may find this overlies a certain peasant cunning. The characters of the *Clochemerle* books are cartoons rather than caricatures. Vaux-en-Beaujolais is said to be the original of Clochemerle; it has a well-known tasting-cellar, the Caveau de Clochemerle, where the local wines can be sampled.

Perhaps it would be more helpful to list the other beaujolais tasting-stations here, rather than scatter them through the text. They are: Beaujeu, Temple de Bacchus; Chazay d'Azergues, Cellier du Baboin; Chénas, Caveau du cru Chénas aux Deschamps; Chiroubles, Terrasse de Chiroubles; Juliénas, Cellier de la Vieille Eglise; Perréon, Caveau de Perréon; Pommiers, Terrasse des Beaujolais; Romanèche, Caveau de l'Union des Viticulteurs du Moulin-à-Vent; Romanèche-Thorins, Caveau du Moulin-à-Vent; St-Jean-d'Ardières, Maison du Beaujolais; St-Lager, Cuvages des Brouilly; Villié-Morgon, Caveau des Morgon.

There is a well-signposted *Route du Beaujolais* that can be followed, though it periodically comes to forks where you must make your decision. If you are not pressed it is well worth while to follow both horns of the dilemma – though, naturally, not at the same time. For those who are hurried (but wine-lovers should never be hurried) there is even a *Route du Beaujolais Rapide*. Perhaps these people are becoming a little over-commercialized.

At St-Amour, in the extreme north of the region, some delectable white wine is made. The nearby fields of Romanèche-Thorins have been mentioned earlier in this chapter.

Hence you pass southward through Juliénas, and Chénas of the generally quick-starting wines. Some of the slopes of Chénas are qualified for the Moulin-à-Vent *appellation* and naturally adopt it. The Domaine des Journets and Domaine des Berthets are outstanding.

Here you have to choose whether to go to Fleurie or Moulin-à-Vent; I recommend both. Fleurie is said to have taken its name from the flowery taste of its wine, but I think this is a piece of rationalization. The single-vineyard Clos de La Rochette is worth looking out for.

Moulin-à-Vent is the aristocrat of the Beaujolais. Its eponymous windmill is sailless and disappointing. Moulin-à-Vent and Romanèche-Thorins used to be considered mâconnais, but their sites are now some way south of the accepted border. The best single-vineyards of Moulin-à-Vent are Clos du Grand Carquelin, Château des Jacques, Clos Rochette, Clos du Champ-Ducour and Grand Clos de Rochegrès.

I have already described Moulin-à-Vent as the most lasting of the beaujolais. Monsieur Jean Thorin jr gave me a Château des Jacques '45 in 1967. When I had rested it after bringing it home it showed no trace of fading, and was full of muscular vitality. Admittedly this was an exceptional year, very slow to develop and correspondingly long-lived.

Now from Moulin-à-Vent you must again select your route, either to Morgon or to Chiroubles. Some of the wines from the hill by Morgon are locally known as the *vins de Py*, which is worth noting, as otherwise you may be puzzled by this if you go to the tasting cellar in the village of Villié-Morgon. An exceptional vineyard is the Château Bellevue.

If you go the other way, to Chiroubles, note the peculiar belfry of the church. Chiroubles wines do not command big prices, but they are unpretentiously enjoyable. From Chiroubles there is yet another choice of directions; but let me finish the big names first, and go on to Brouilly and its superior Côte. There is a tasting cellar for the Brouillys in the village of St-Lager. You see another peculiar rock formation here, Mont Brouilly; the vineyards near this are the Côte de Brouilly, and the others (slightly less appreciated) are Brouilly *tout simple*. There is a chapel of Notre Dame on the top of Mont Brouilly, to which the *vignerons* make pilgrimages of prayer and thanksgiving.

The other way from Chiroubles leads to Beaujeu, an interesting place, though I do not rank its wines very highly.

For this was the ancient capital of the Beaujolais, and it gives its name to one of the earliest baronies of France. Also there is an Hospice here too, with its own annual charity sale of the wines from the vineyards that have been given for the support of the old and the sick. Here, as at Beaune (Chapter 12), the auction is a *vente à la chandelle*. The most famous vineyard belonging to the Hospice is a Brouilly-Pisse-Vieille, into the etymology of which name I do not propose to delve in these chaste pages. The other Hospice vineyards are all classified as beaujolais *Villages*.

From here you work south to Villefranche-sur-Saône, the present chief town of the Beaujolais, which is full of wine and wraps the visitor in a pleasant winey bouquet; but we have left the region of the best growths and are approaching the Lyonnais. Some writers extend the Beaujolais almost to the suburbs of Lyon, but this Bas Beaujolais is an area of earthy, undistinguished products – too many of which, I should guess, come to British and American hotels and restaurants.

Villefranche, incidentally, is the headquarters of the *Compagnons de Beaujolais*, an organization modelled on the *Confrérie des Chevaliers du Tastevin* (see Chapter 12).

On this tour you should arrange to arrive at Thoissey one mealtime, where the Chapon Fin (M. Blanc) has two stars in Michelin. It is about opposite Romanèche-Thorins, a few miles east across the Saône. On the outskirts of Romanèche there is an attractive inn, Les Maritonnes (M. Fauvin) with a good table, and a room (preferably on the side away from the railway line) makes a good base for touring the Beaujolais.

Now we come to beaujolais *blanc*, become increasingly popular and increasingly reinforced by what is really mâcon *blanc*. (But see p. 110 concerning the present confused situation of St-Véran.)

There is some confusion as to the grape used for this. The old books speak of it as an *aligoté* wine, and this was true when its making was confined mostly to the south of the Beaujolais.

But most beaujolais *blanc* that is shipped now comes from the northern area, near the Mâconnais, and is made of *chardonnay* or *pinot blanc*, or a blend of these. *Aligoté* is tolerated by the *AC* rules, but if you want a beaujolais *aligoté* now – according to S. P. E. Simon, who made a thorough research into this question for his authoritative articles in the *Wine and Spirit Trade Record* – you will have to look for it at the *comptoirs* of cafés in the Lyonnais. This beaujolais *aligoté* is an acceptable carafe wine, particularly if it is 'improved' with a percentage of *chardonnay*. But it cannot compare for quality with the beaujolais *chardonnay*.

The best of the latter is made from fields adjoining the Mâconnais Pouilly-Fuissé. Château de Loyse is a *cru* that I esteem, made between St-Amour and Pontanevaux on *RN* 6. The vineyard goes back to the seventeenth century. There is another good beaujolais *blanc*, too, at St-Amour. Other good wine comes from some way further south, round Lachassagne, where the château belongs to the family of the Marquis de Laguiche, of Montrachet fame.

There are some white wines made in the Bas Beaujolais from the *gamay noir à jus blanc*, but these are not entitled to the *appellation* of beaujolais *supérieur blanc*, nor even, strictly, to that of beaujolais *blanc*.

Vin rosé is made in the Beaujolais, and even some *vin gris*, kept pale by the very brief contact of the skins with the juice. Consumed on a hot day, a few miles at most from the places where they are made, these are palatable thirst-quenchers.

Such then is beaujolais, an undemanding wine for all purposes, unfortunately much abused in export and even within France. But there are reasonable hopes of these malpractices becoming controlled in the near future.

On the basis of quality Chablis should really have been considered immediately after the Côte d'Or, but it has been convenient to run on down from that Côte through the Chalonnais, Mâconnais and Beaujolais, particularly as some of the vineyards on their borders overlap each other. Now I am wafted back, on fumes of wine, over a hundred miles north from Villefranche and a little west, to yet another town that lives on vinting. There is a delectable, traffic-free by-road from Beaune, via Bligny, Pouilly-en-Auxois (not -Fuissé), St-Thibault, Semur, Epoisses (home of the famous cheese), Guillon and Noyers to Chablis. Often it runs beside the Burgundian canal, and in places there are mile-long hedges of laburnum.

The first thing to say about chablis is that it is the wine that never was. The Chablis field is anyhow one of the smallest of fine wine-producing areas. Its output is further restricted by a hazardous climate, and the local necessity of resting the land for longer-than-average periods. Genuine chablis is therefore rare even in fine years, when the *AC* output-restrictions are relaxed. There may be about 650,000 bottles of *grands* and 1st *crus*, 1,500,000 of chablis and 1,800,000 of petit chablis. But much of the last never reaches the bottle, being sold in the wood to bars and cafés, in the half-sized barrels known as *feuillettes*, for the carafe trade.

Where then does all the chablis come from that you find in the wine-list of every provincial hotel and restaurant? Long before the 1966 controversy broke, about the mis-titling of burgundy, it was recognized by all but the least sophisticated that three quarters of the stuff sold as chablis was not genuine.

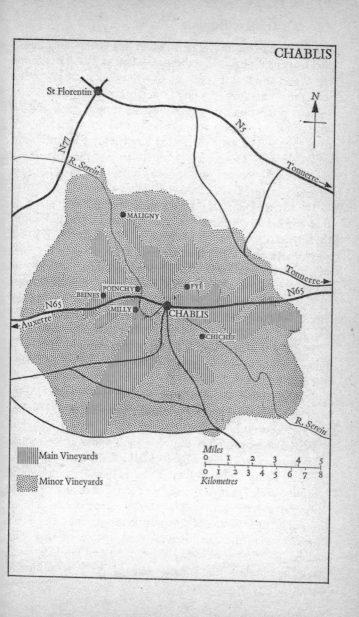

It may or may not have been decent dry wine. The point is that real chablis has a very distinctive flavour that is not found elsewhere, and that if you want this you do not wish to drink something else, however good, under the same name.

Your protection is to drink only the named *grands* and 1st *crus*, and if you cannot afford these and must confine yourself to chablis and/or petit chablis, to buy it only from the most reputable wine-merchants. If at a restaurant the named *crus* are too costly for me, or not even represented, then I choose instead a *bourgogne*, mâcon or beaujolais *blanc*.

The town of Chablis is hardly more than a large village, so that when you go there you are impressed more indeed by the size of its output rather than by its paucity. It is not a particularly attractive place, though it has a romantic gate; still, it has the peculiar fascination of a headquarters of peasant-proprietor wine-making, with all the character that this evokes in the inhabitants. Chablis has an excellent restaurant at the Hôtel de l'Etoile (M. Bergerand), as a further justification for a visit.

Much of the wine here is stored in over-ground *chais*, as at Puligny, in contrast to most of Burgundy which has deep cellars.

The little river Serein trickles through the township, with the choice vineyards on its right bank, facing south and (somewhat exceptionally, this) south-west.

I have eschewed science in this book, but it is interesting that the vineyards lie on what is called a Kimmeridgian ridge, after our Kimmeridge in Dorset, one of the very rare belts of bituminous clay that geologists have found. I cannot trace the history of any vineyards in Dorset, though we once had them in most of the counties of southern England; but if there had been such they would presumably have given a wine like chablis. For the chablis grapes are those of the other good white burgundies, and it is the soil that gives it its elusive quality.

Unhappily Chablis suffers far more even than the rest of Burgundy from destructive frosts in the spring. It lies high, about 1350 feet above sea-level, and also attracts violent hailstorms in the summer. Indeed, the top-soil of the slopes is often washed away, and has to be carried back and patiently redistributed by hand, which certainly calls for devotion on the part of the growers. Even in such a fine and prolific year elsewhere as 1945 there was virtually no wine made in Chablis (due to severe frost), and the '51, '53, '60, '61, '65 and '67 harvests were miserably small. The '53s and '61s, so good elsewhere, were a great loss. One may say that a bad year for the Côte d'Or will certainly be worse for Chablis, and that even a good year for the Côte d'Or may still be bad for Chablis.

The Chablis wine-fields, like others in Burgundy, used to be dotted with curious contraptions, looking as if they had been designed by Emett or Rube Goldberg, that were used as anti-hail cannons. Fortunately, from the aesthetic point of view, these proved to be ineffectual, and the only remedy for hail was found to be that of insurance. But frost has been shown to be less irresistible, and any tour round the Chablis vineyards will show you numerous different heating devices about whose efficiency the proprietors will argue as fiercely as about the respective standings of the wines.

Another Chablis difficulty is the quick exhaustion of the soil here. The text-books say that fields have to be rested for up to twenty years. However I was assured locally that, with improved methods of fertilization, this is no longer true. Fields do have to lie fallow, so that properties will rarely be entirely productive at any given time. But, I was told, a well-cared for plot would produce satisfactorily for as much as forty years. With this and other improvements the graph marking the five-year average of chablis output is showing an encouraging rise. But it remains, and always will, a scanty harvest.

I have also read old text-books that condemn the local

practice of training the vines on wires that follow the contours of the slopes. Their austere writers claim that this has led to some deterioration of quality. I can only say that no one whom I met in Chablis remembered the vines growing without support, and indeed this method prevails all over Burgundy, except with the *gamay* in the Beaujolais.

The classification of chablis was fixed in 1938. (The word 'cru', not 'cuvée', has always been used here.) There are *grands* and 1st *crus*; then comes chablis, and finally petit chablis. The *grands crus* are the best vineyards of the *communes* of Chablis, Milly and Poinchy. The yield, by strict *AC* rules, must not exceed 1877 bottles per acre and the alcohol must not fall below 11°, another of the many local difficulties in such a climate.

The 1st *crus* come from vineyards in the same *communes*, but slightly less favoured by nature, and in Beines, Chichée (charming name), Fyé and Maligny. The yield must not exceed 2170 bottles per acre and the alcohol must not fall below 10.5°. If in a poor year a *grand* or 1st *cru* cannot make the necessary alcoholic strength the wine must be sold just as petit chablis.

The wine known just as chablis comes from any of the twenty *communes* of the area, but there is the same restriction of output, though the alcohol need only reach 10°; also the grapes, as in the case of the *grand* and 1st *crus*, must be the *chardonnay*, locally called the *beaunois*. Finally, petit chablis (9°) must come from the delimited area; however, not only is there no effective restriction of output, but also any grapes can be used provided they are not from ungrafted grape briars. In most years all chablis needs sugaring, and in some years quite a lot; but this should not be done to the extent of overcoming its dry, flinty taste.

The *grands crus*, in alphabetic order, are Blanchots, Bougros, Clos, Grenouilles, Preuses, Valmur and Vaudésir. Of these I suppose the last has the greatest reputation, but I have a personal *faible* for Grenouilles which, without losing any of the distinctive characteristics of chablis, seems to be slightly softer than the others. It is, so to speak, the feminine wine of Chablis. In the case of any of them a *Mise du Domaine* label, if you can find it, will assure enhanced satisfaction. But the *grand cru* vineyards are divided among numerous owners, and there is nothing wrong if you find these fine wines bottled by different shippers.

There is also a small proprietary vineyard, about 3 acres in extent, called La Moutonne, which after much argument has been ranked as a *grand cru*. (Note the *La*, and be careful about bottles labelled 'chablis-Moutonne'.) When I was there in 1967 it seemed to be in poor shape but I have had samples of the '69 and '70 vintages which were quite good. Altogether these *grand cru* vineyards only amount to 90 acres.

There are rather a lot of 1st *crus*, on both banks of the Serein, so it will be convenient to group them by *communes*: in Beines – Clos-de-Troême; in Chablis – Beugnons, Butteaux, Châtains, Forêts, Lys, Mélinots, Montmains, Roncières, Séché, Vaillons (also, to confuse matters, called Roncières); in Chichée – Vaucoupin, Vaugiraud (also spelled in several similar ways) and Vosgros; in Fyé – Châpelots, Montée-de-Tonnerre (an appropriate name here), Monts de Milieu and Pied-d'Aloup; in Milly – Côte de Léchet; and in Poinchy – Boroy (also spelled Beaurroy), Côte de Fontenay, Fourchaume, Vaulorent and Vaupulent. Fourchaume and Lys are the ones that I have seen most often in English wine-lists, but all that I know make fine wine in any year when the weather gives them a chance, and all are worth trying.

The multiplicity of these 1st *cru* vineyards has led to some confusion, and they have recently been grouped under seven main titles, Côte de Léchet, Fourchaume, Montée-de-Tonnerre, Monts de Milieu, Montmains, Vaillons and Vaucoupin. However, proprietors are permitted to use the vineyard name if they wish; thus a Fontenay can be sold either as

Côte de Fontenay or as Fourchaume. The idea of this is to allow blendings of different 1st *crus*, often necessitated by the small output, to be sold with a local name instead of just as an anonymous '1st *cru*'.

There are also various named vineyards outside the official classification of 1st *crus* which have some reputation; these are, in Chablis – Chalevaux, Champlains, Epinottes, Vaugerlans and Vaupinet; in Chichée – Dessous-le-Bois-de-Serre, Haut-des-Vaux-Noyers, Montaigus; in Maligny – L'Homme-Mort; and in Poinchy – Benfer, Quatre-Chemins and Vallée-des-Vaux. But their wines are rarely exported under their own names, so they are not of importance to us.

Nothing in the foregoing is to be construed (as the lawyers say) as implying that chablis and petit chablis bottlings are not good, when genuine. I have enjoyed Avery's Chablis Villages, from *vignobles secondaires*, nicely chilled, as a disingenuous little wine for a good swig when I am thirsty. (This old *appellation*, Chablis Villages, is no longer used in France.) There is also a *vin de consommation courante* made round Chablis from the *sacy* grape, which I tested recently in an *estaminet* near Auxerre. It was quite fair. I am not aware of the continued production of any red chablis though I daresay some critic could find an odd patch to confound me. But it was not uncommon before the fields were reduced by two-thirds after the phylloxera. Some of King John's and Henry VIII's Auxerre may well have been red chablis.

Chablis wine is light in colour, a pale gold with glints of green. Except in great years its bouquet is slight, but it is always refined. Its taste is fresh and clean; I have already spoken of it as flinty, but others call it steely. In unenlightened periods of warfare, before the age of half-track carriers and helicopters, when infantrymen had to march twenty miles a day with sixty pounds of equipment on their backs, I remember learning to suck pebbles on the trek in hot weather. Chablis has an underlying touch of that taste. This stony flavour, together with its strawlike colour and elegant bouquet, are the qualities of real chablis that show up the imitations.

It comes on fast, but is rather sharp at first and I do not recommend drinking the *grands crus* until they are approaching the age of three – say, take a '70 vintage, which at present is promising, in the summer of '73. A 1st *cru* can be enjoyed at eighteen months, chablis or petit chablis at a year. Four-chaume is reputed to be a very quick starter, Monts-de-Milieu a slow one. Most of chablis fades after five or six years, but a fine year of a fine field will last up to ten. I had half a magnum of Valmur '29 at an oyster feast shortly before the outbreak of the Second World War; it showed no trace of fatigue – though I myself may have done at the end of the meal, which was capped by Stilton and fine old tawny. In 1960 I shared a bottle of Vaudésir '47 (a great year in Chablis, with uncharacteristically big wines) with a knowledgeable friend who insisted that it was not yet at its best. A Blanchots '59 that M. Rémon opened for me in May 1967 was at the top of its form. But these were exceptions; the first two, also, were years that ran up to 14° alcohol. If you are lucky enough to have veritable chablis regularly available to you you should not ordinarily chance it beyond the sixth year.

Grands crus and 1st *crus* should be kept by the shippers in oak casks till bottled, but there is said to be no objection to storing chablis and petit chablis in large metal or cement tanks, suitably lined; some shippers even say that these small wines gain by being matured in large containers.

Chablis goes well with the delicate fishes, particularly shell-fish and most particularly oysters. (I personally think it is even better with natives than with the more pungent French, Dutch or Portuguese.) But it will not stand up to full sauces. If you are going to have your lobster *cardinal* or *américaine*, still more if you are going to have it *thermidor*, you need a fuller wine. But it is admirable with plain grilled lobster *maître d'hôtel*, or a cold lobster with a light mayonnaise or *sauce verte*.

Some gourmets even think it is overwhelmed by salmon. I certainly consider it can accompany what they call salmon trout.

It is a beautiful wine for cooking, too. The local *écrevisses au chablis* are famous, and it imparts its delicate flavour in the vessel to either veal or chicken.

But although it is a good accompaniment, and ingredient, I am not sure whether it is not better to drink it by itself, when nothing obtrudes on its clean, delicate dryness. A half-bottle as an aperitif before lunch in summer-time, even if necessary a half-bottle shared, induces a grateful mood in which to approach a light meal. And it is a lovely drink after dinner, on a warm night, taken just for refreshment, as is, in my opinion, the proper use of German wines.

12. The Hospices de Beaune and the Confrérie des Chevaliers du Tastevin

Every traveller through Burgundy, though he may pass by the Domaine de la Romanée-Conti or the vineyard of Le Montrachet, must surely have stopped for at least a few minutes at the Hôtel Dieu at Beaune, generally known as the Hospices. (It is in the plural because the trustees administer another charitable institution, for children, elsewhere in the town.)

I cannot recall how many times I have parked in the *grande place* of Beaune (though it is getting more difficult to find space now), turned the corner and passed through the gateway to the Cour d'Honneur of the Hospices. Always it is thrilling to see this masterpiece of late Gothic architecture and reflect on its endowment; to satisfy one's aesthetic and historical senses and recognize their object as a charity nourished on wine.

It is true that the charity was originally much impugned. Nicolas Rolin, who founded the Hôtel Dieu in 1443, was chancellor of Burgundy under Philip the Good. Now chancellors are rarely popular with their contemporaries, but Rolin's extortions seem to have attracted an unusual measure of obloquy. One of the typical comments was that of the king of France, Louis XI, who remarked that 'having made so many people poor and homeless he could well afford to make his peace with the Almighty by providing for some of them'. Fifty old people still live in the noble almshouse, sixty orphans are cared for and educated, and the poor of Beaune are eligible for nursing.

Looking across the courtyard one sees the lovely four-storied façade topped by its dormered roof of patterned polychrome Burgundian tiles. One passes the lovely well-head and mounts the staircase to see the famous polyptych of Rogier van der Weyden, one of the masterpieces of early Flemish painting, commissioned by the founder himself. The old pharmacy is still full of the original blue and white vases for medieval remedies, and of ancient pewter mortars and pestles. (Of course there is a modern pharmacy too, and an operating theatre, and other contemporary facilities.) And in the kitchen cooking is still done with antique utensils, over log-fires that burn in huge Gothic chimney-pieces.

In the great ward the old folk doze in curtained cubicles that give them a measure of privacy, but the hangings can be drawn back so that even the bedridden can see the elevation of the host when mass is celebrated. The gracious nursing sisters work at their devoted tasks, still wearing the wimples and long robes of the period of the foundation; and one reflects that the unhygienic consequences of these may be offset by the psychological effect, on the patients, of this maintenance of tradition. Like sailors when they go south, the sisters change from blue garments in winter to white in summer.

The Hospices were enlarged with another courtyard in the seventeenth century, but in a sympathetic style. And in the last court one comes to the ancient press-room and cellars which are the proper subject of this book.

For what distinguishes this benefaction from many such is that Rolin and his wife, Guigone de Salins, endowed the Hospices in perpetuity with their own private vineyards, and so encouraged others, in the course of the Hospices' long history, to follow this practical example, down to Maurice Drouhin, the shipper, who in our own time bequeathed some of his finest Beaune vineyards to this famous charity.

From Rolin's age the wines of the Hospices' *crus* have supported his foundation. Originally the sales were by private treaty. But over a hundred years ago, in 1851, the first of the now celebrated annual auctions was held. Till recently these were conducted in the Hospices, and splendid ancient tapestries belonging to the charity were brought out to decorate the courtyard for the event. But now the crowd of buyers, would-be buyers and interested spectators has become too great for the accommodation, and the sale has been moved to the closed market of the town, a less romantic location, even when decorated with the famous tapestries, but more commodious.

The auction regularly takes place on the third Sunday in November, though in 1965 it had to be postponed on account of the lateness of the vintage in that year. (There was also an unfortunate clash of dates with another occurrence, the Presidential election.) The wines, obviously, are then so young that only the most expert can evaluate them. There are twenty-four red and eight white important vineyards that have been bequeathed to the Hospices, all of them in the Côte de Beaune, but not all in the *commune* of Beaune. These scattered vineyards cover rather more than 125 acres in all, and their income provides for the entire maintenance of the Hospices. The wines are named after the individuals who left the vineyards. The most famous of the reds are those called after the founders, Nicolas Rolin and Guigone de Salins; others that command almost as high prices are Dames Hospitalières, Billardet and Dr Peste – an unfortunate name, as has been pointed out, for one of his profession. The *cuvée* Loppin is the most famous white. Other celebrated vineyards are Charlotte Dumay, Jehan de Massol, Blondeau and Jehan Humblot. The entire list of the principal *crus* is given in Appendix C.

Tasting takes place, the day before the sale, in the cellar. There is a high fee for attending this, and tickets for the auction are also costly and difficult to get. The wines were originally sold by the *queue*, but this practice has been abandoned and they are now sold in lots of so many *pièces* (nominally 304 bottles each, though the eventual output is closer to

290). They are sold *à la chandelle*; that is, the last bid before the candle goes out wins the lot. This is not, apparently, a very satisfactory method, though hallowed by tradition. There are often disputes by disappointed bidders, and the lots then have to be put up again.

The prices are very high, not only because the wines are usually extremely well-made and because of the charitable motives involved; there is also the incentive of publicity, like that of the butchers bidding for the prize-winners at London's Smithfield Fat Cattle Show. This exaggerates the values, because many merchants and restaurateurs like to be able to offer their clients Hospices wine. In 1966 the auction of 752 *pièces* (wine for about 218,000 bottles) fetched the record sum of over £200,000 (taking the exchange at the level then prevailing), or the equivalent of more than over 18s. 6d. per bottle absolute wholesale, before any other expense besides the growing and vinification has been incurred. In 1961, a great year, it was on the same basis over 23s. a bottle. In the last decade the prices have risen even more steeply, though the mediocrity of the '68 vintage, and the abundance of the '70, did cause welcome reductions per *pièce*; only for '71 to show a yet more sensational advance. In this, the last year for which the figures were available as I wrote, the 341 *pièces* sold for 2,928,100 francs, over £2 a bottle, and Nicolas Rolin fetched £6 a bottle – at the Hospices. Even the white Corton Charlemagne – a wine which I do not find as outstanding as it used to be – touched £5·50.

Avery's of Bristol have perhaps the best selection of Hospices wines in England, and their lowest price (in their winter 1972/3 catalogue) is £3·94 a bottle for the '64s and '66s, and their highest (for the splendid Dr Peste '64) is £5·51. You can imagine at what price such wines will be quoted in restaurant wine-lists. Meanwhile more recent vintages will have gone still higher, still more now the effect is felt of Value Added Tax.

But there is a guarantee of quality. The vinification at the *cuverie* behind the Hôtel Dieu has all the conscientiousness of ancient tradition, and when the vintage does not reach a reasonable standard (as in 1956) the auction is suppressed and the wine sold off by private treaty. I think this should have been done in 1968 also.

The output of the vineyards varies greatly, according to the season. In 1965, for example, there were only 294 *pièces*; in 1970 there were 679. The average is 157,000 bottles – before any ullage. This indicates the precariousness of Burgundian vintages.

Unfortunately the somewhat emotionally exaggerated prices achieved by the Hospices wines affect not only the price-levels of neighbouring wines of similar quality, but have a tendency also to set standards for the whole of the good areas of Burgundy, even in the Côte de Nuits. 'My wine is as good as that Hospices parcel,' says the maker, 'why should I sell it for less?' Thus what is necessarily a dear wine becomes artificially dearer. Even if they do not affect all vineyards, the coefficients of the Hospices' auction prices from year to year establish comparative values for the different vintages – at a time when the future of the still-fermenting growths can only be guessed at.

There are, by the way, popular, inexpensive tastings of non-Hospices' wines from all over Burgundy, held simultaneously in the outbuildings of the *hôtel de ville*, exhibitions by various shippers, a procession of floats, dancing and a general atmosphere of fête. And the exciting day ends with *dîner aux chandelles* set in one of the bastions of the city walls. But this forms part of the second section of this chapter.

In 1933 the burgundy trade was in a parlous condition. There had been three wretched vintages in succession, from 1930 to 1932. The *AC* regulations had not yet been published, to give confidence to such buyers as there were; and after four years of the world-slump few buyers anyhow were coming forward. Then a group of Burgundian gourmets and winemen, local patriots all, headed by the late Camille Rodier and Georges Faiveley, came forward with a far-sighted and successful promotion scheme which, unlike many such, was of great public benefit.

Meeting first in a cellar at Nuits, as if it were some secret conspiracy, they organized the *Confrérie des Chevaliers du Tastevin* (the 's' in *Tastevin* is silent), with a chapter of officers with ancient titles, provided with medieval robes and with a dramatic ritual. The brothers were to be of three ranks, *chevaliers*, *commandeurs* and *grands officiers*, according to their standing in the wine-world and their knowledge particularly of burgundy. The brotherhood was named after the traditional Burgundian tasting cup, which is of irregularly fluted and dimpled silver, to show the colour and clarity of the wine being tested, even by candlelight in the cellar. The tasting cup of the order is slung, for the dignification of the *Confrères*, on a fine moiré ribbon, its end beautifully mitred, of scarlet and gold.

The organization acquired, for its headquarters, the sixteenth-century Cistercian Château de Clos Vougeot, whose brothers contributed so much to the development of Burgundian viticulture. The buildings were erected by Dom Jean Loysier, forty-eighth abbot of Cîteaux, and incorporated the much more ancient press-room and cellars. By the nineteenth century, they were in a ruinous condition, till they were restored in 1891 – in the taste of the time – by a Monsieur Bocquet, a proprietor at Savigny. By the members' subscriptions, by profits on its banquets and publications, and by gifts from enthusiasts (in which respect the Americans have been particularly generous), the *Confrérie* has largely returned the famous buildings to their original appearance, and will eventually do so completely. By prizes and publicity the

Court of the Order has stimulated the publication of numerous monographs on burgundy and gastronomy.

In addition to its regular series of banquets, the *Confrérie* from time to time holds extraordinary *chapîtres* for special purposes, such as that for the company of the Comédie Française, which gave a performance of *Tartuffe* in the courtyard of the château before dinner. After Rabelais, Molière is the chief literary model of the organization.

It now has numerous sub-chapters in the United States, and some in Australia and the former French African colonies; but none as yet in Great Britain, though it has numerous British members. It has been much imitated in other wine-producing areas; indeed there is scarcely any in France that has not by now created a similar organization, though one takes leave to doubt whether all of them are of sufficient importance to justify this. If there is any criticism of the *Confrérie* it is that it has been too liberal in extending its membership to the famous, and even the notorious, regardless of their knowledge of wine. But perhaps I am being churlish.

How handsome the floodlit château looked on the winter night in 1959 as I approached it down the sacred *route des grands crus*, to be 'enthroned' as a *chevalier*. On arrival, we postulants and our sponsors assembled in one of the rooms of the group of buildings, and at about 7 p.m. the halberdiers and trumpeters of the *Confrérie*, in red and gold uniforms, preceded the chapter, in their long scarlet robes and high doctoral hats, into the room. Four men in hunting costume then played a fanfare on horns, and the first of the innumerable *allocutions* was given. Then in turn each of the candidates for promotion or admission was called up, and his qualifications were cited. In turn each took the oath of fidelity to burgundy (which I mentally assumed was not to be an exclusive fidelity), and each was dubbed on the shoulder with a vine-root, while the *Grand Chancellier* addressed him in ancient French. Then the candidate was kissed on (or near) both cheeks by the Grand

Master (heavily moustached at the time of my initiation), was girt with the appropriate ribbon with its silver *tastevin* attached, and invited to sign the book of honour with a quill pen.

When the list had been gone through we adjourned to partake of *bourgogne cassis*, in another room. We inspected the château and its vast thirteenth-century presses. And, '*à 20 heures précises*', as the invitation stated – that is, about 8.30, we took our seats in the vast cellar for dinner. Hanging on each of its pillars were leather baskets, formerly strung on the backs of the grape-pickers and now decorated with medieval arms and their respective dates: one went back to the early twelfth century.

There were about 600 covers; we had six courses, and several servings each of six different wines; and it seemed like sixty speeches, very much in the French tradition and some of them rather Rabelaisian, blessedly interspersed with the *grivois* songs of the *Cadets de Bourgogne* seated on a platform over which hung the banner of the order with its motto, *Jamais en vain, toujours en vin*. The *Cadets* are a choir of *vignerons*, admirable natural musicians, whose weather-beaten faces proclaim their calling. In their white shirts, black sleeveless jackets and black trousers, they look like figures out of some old Flemish painting of a *kermesse*. Their choruses are accompanied by a peculiar rhythmic clapping, the *ban bourgignon*, on the part of the audience. These intermissions provide salutary pauses between the courses, which enable one to keep going. For it was 1 a.m. before we rose, and 2 a.m. when I got back to my room in Dijon.

A typical dinner begins with the traditional procession of chefs and kitchen-hands carrying the cold sucking-pigs flanked with *jambon persillé à la dijonnaise*. Pots of the finest Dijon mustard are circulated; I was dubious, the first time, about the effect of this on the wine, but the locals should know, and at any rate it aids digestion, a valid consideration for such a meal. The next three courses are brought really hot – a notable achievement for a dinner of nearly 600 covers served in a cellar. Finally there is always a reproduction of one of the great presses of the château made of nougatine, surrounded by marzipan and ice cream in the form of Burgundian snails.

Here, as a sample, is the menu and wine-list of the *Chapître du Printemps*, 1967, at which I was promoted *Commandeur* of the order:

PREMIÈRE ASSIETTE

Les Gentils Porcelets en leur Gelée & le Jambon Persillé Dijonnaise
relevés de bonne Moutarde Forte de Dijon
escortés d'un Bourgogne Aligoté 1964 frais et gouleyant
de Magny-les-Villers

DEUXIÈME ASSIETTE

Les Soufflés de Brochet Truffés Nantua
humidifiés d'un Puligny-Montrachet 1964 subtil et bouqueté
'Combettes'

ETREMETS

La Fricassée de Coquelets aux Morilles
accompagnée d'un Beaune 1962 soyeaux et prenant

DORURE

Les Jambons Rôtis Printaniers
arrosés d'un Nuits Clos de la Maréchale 1964 suave et caressant

ISSUE DE TABLE

Le Véritable Comté et ses Compagnons Froumigiers d'Ailleurs
rehaussés d'un Clos de la Roche 1962 de mémorable lignée

BOUTEHORS

Le Pressoir du Clos de Vougeot en Nougatine
Les Escargots en Glace – Les Massepains Bourguignons
Les Fraises de Meuilley en Melba
Café Noir & Chaud, Le Vieux Marc, la Prunelle de Bourgogne
fort idoines à stimuler vapeurs subtiles du cerveau

The catering was done by M. Fargeau, *patron* of the Croix-Blanche at Nuits-St-Georges.

The medieval uniforms, the evocation of the past in the citations, and the antique language of the menu might tend, it could be thought, to seem a trifle silly, even in the euphoria of wine; but it is not so. Jules Romains wrote, after the *chapître* that he attended:

... the diners evidence what one may call an affecting kind of happiness – that is to say, a will to believe in life, in its pleasures, of which burgundy is one of the most effective: and to continue to hold this belief in spite of the trials and threats with which this age never ceases to inflict us. There is a magnificent ceremonial relieved by witty burlesque which Molière might have been proud to inspire; and the eloquence of the speeches combines literary culture with a lively local patriotism. The whole forms, for one evening, a kind of shield to protect the *joie de vivre* that we can still experience.

Women are admitted to the order, and woman guests welcomed. In my recollection half at least of these were chic, which is a high proportion anywhere; and here and there one sees a type – not chic indeed, but something much more interesting – who seems a pure Toulouse-Lautrec character coming from the Parisian music halls of the 1890s. These are undoubtedly the ones who best understand burgundy.

On the occasion of my last visit I noted the splendid progress made in the restoration of the château. The renaissance sculptures have been replaced over the great entrance, which itself has been restored to its original form. Thanks to the American *commanderies* the reception room has been entirely renewed. Some more intimate domestic improvements have been effected, not so important perhaps in summer but doubtless appreciated on icy winter nights, which remove the necessity of crossing a vast open courtyard to visit the lavatories. The restoration of the room above the great cellar, which will become the chapter house of the order, was substantially advanced.

I think the first thing an Englishman notices at these dinners is the youth of the wines that are served. But there would not be enough old wine to serve 600 covers so liberally, several times in the year. And the wines themselves exemplify what I said in Chapter 1 about burgundy – that it is not, in its natural condition and as drunk in Burgundy itself, a heavy wine. This is what justifies their service of red wine with ham.

The greatest sessions of the *Confrérie* take place at the November weekend known as *Les Trois Glorieuses*, named after the three historic but subsequently disillusionizing days of 1830 that saw the change of dynasty in Paris. There is first, on the Saturday night, a dinner at Clos Vougeot similar to that which I have described. Next comes the dinner at Beaune, after the auction of the Hospices wines. This is held by candle-light also, in the depths of a bastion of the town walls, flanking the Hospices. The twin cellars are decorated with flags and tapestries and coats of arms. The menu aims to reproduce, in miniature, one of the ancient banquets of the Dukes of Burgundy. Here is a typical list of courses: *consommé à la mode d'Auxois*, hot *pâté* of thrush, fillets of pike cooked with grapes, salmis of guinea-fowl cooked in Beaune wine, roast ham *forestière*, Burgundian cheeses and an extraordinary selection of *petit fours* and other sweets. The wines run the gamut of Burgundy, and the courses are broken by the amusing songs of the *Joyeux Bourguignons*. Finally, on the Monday, comes the luncheon, lasting all the afternoon, of the *Paulée* at Meursault. (*Paulée* is a local word of disputed etymology meaning the midday pause of the workers in the vineyard.)

This last function differs from the others in that it is the vineyard-owners, great and small, who organize the meal and bring their own bottles for the delectation of their personal guests and their own reward. These bottles are usually not labelled with the name and date of some famous *cru*, but are precious survivors from the private reserves of the hosts' own cellars set aside for this occasion. A prize of 100 bottles of

Meursault is offered annually for the best book on Burgundy – not just on its wine, but also on the life, scenery and architecture of this proud province.

Only the best food and wine will carry the human constitution through the triple test of the *Trois Glorieuses*. And it must be remembered that the most important participants in these events will have been working hard the while, tasting and buying professionally, with their pockets and reputation dependent on their endurance.

The *Confrérie* publishes a semi-annual journal which, in addition to recording its proceedings, contains much informative wine-lore. (For instance, one issue revealed to me the writing of Baudelaire on wine, on which subject the poet was as sound as on painting.) And it organizes an annual impartial blind tasting of new wines submitted by numerous growers (many of them small men) from the *communes* not only of the Côte d'Or but of all Burgundy. The judgements of this *Tastevinage*, distributed to members, form a most helpful guide to the amateur in the restocking of his cellar.

This *Tastevinage* is an examination, not a competition. No attempt is made to rank the accepted wines in order of merit. A bottle is passed, or rejected; if passed, the makers may quote this on its labels, which forms a valuable endorsement, justifying an increase of price. But the examination is rigorous. At the 1966 tasting, for example, though all the wines had been submitted to a preliminary test before reaching the final jury, only 166 out of the 251 different burgundies were finally granted the accolade, and at the 1967 tasting only 180 out of the 257 different burgundies were passed. (Both are about the average percentage.) And it must be realized that the wines are passed in relation to their vintage; thus a wine *tasteviné* from 1965, say, will not be likely to be as good as one similarly endorsed from 1961. Also quite modest wines, *aligotés* for instance, may be *tastevinés* if outstanding in their class.

The strictness of the test is further demonstrated by the fact that, though there is no entrance fee for the *Tastevinage*, a sum is charged for each *tasteviné* label used by the shippers for the wines that are passed, so it would pay a commercial body to be less exacting in its scrutiny. But it must also be made clear that many makers of fine wine do not think they need this endorsement. Therefore, while a *tasteviné* label will always guarantee a good bottle, of its kind, the absence of such a label implies no demerit in the wine – which rests on the reputation of its vineyard or *commune* and of its shippers.

Apart from this the *Confrérie* receives no subvention from the trade. It is self-financing and absolutely independent – unlike certain trade associations in which, as the Grand Camerlingue M. René Engel has said, '*le mot "servir" se traduirait, trop souvent, par "se servir"*'.

The *Confrérie* also holds a picturesque religious celebration on 24 January, on the day of St Vincent, patron saint of *vignerons*, each year in a different Burgundian parish. The local inhabitants decorate their streets as a triumphal way, and join the representatives of other villages, carrying their respective banners. There is a mass in the church, with a sermon from some member of the local hierarchy calling on the participants not just to glory in the fruit of their own laborious efforts, but to realize their wine as one of the greatest gifts of God.

So in various ways the *Confrérie* proceeds with its beneficent task, not only of restoring the historic building which is the greatest surviving monument of the ancient Burgundian wine trade, but also of carrying on, for future generations, the prestigious heritage of its fascinating, much abused but – in the proper hands – wholly delectable wine.

13. Sparkling Burgundy, Vin Rosé, Marc de Bourgogne, etc.

I must confess that I cannot recall ever having drunk sparkling red burgundy before starting this book. I had heard that it was a useful medium for relaxing the inhibitions of young ladies in the provinces, but had not had any occasion to put this to the test. However, since undertaking my contract with the publishers, I have, with proper conscientiousness, tested several bottles of different brands and found them quite unobjectionable, if not very interesting.

To qualify as sparkling burgundy under *AC* rules at least 30% of the wine must come from noble grapes – which phrase includes the good *gamay à jus blanc* for sparkling red wine coming from the Beaujolais. The balance may consist of *bourgogne grand ordinaire* or, for the white, of *aligoté*. The higher the percentage of noble grapes, the better the wine – up to a point. For I am told that pure *chardonnay* juice does not make as good a *sparkling* white burgundy as a mixture mostly of *chardonnay* with a proportion of *aligoté*. Some of the sparkling white burgundies are made almost entirely of white grapes, and are thus the equivalent of a *blanc de blancs* – much lighter than the ordinary bottlings, but quite elegant if not excessively sugared.

Also under *AC* rules the champenization method must be employed. After the first fermentation in the vats the wine must be bottled and the bottles stored neck downwards (*mise sur pointes*) to await the second fermentation in bottle. The bottles must be twisted regularly to force the sediment down towards the neck. They must be disgorged (*dégorgement*) of their impurities and topped up with similar wine plus as much sugar as is needed to give them the degree of sweetening required. This sweetening matter (*liqueur d'expédition*) must be pure sugar melted in wine. Then the final corking must be effected, and the corks secured with wire. Sparkling burgundy may not be legally offered for sale, in France, within nine months of the secondary fermentation. This of course is a very short period in comparison with the bottle-age of good champagne. But the best brands of sparkling burgundy are usually kept in the cellars for from twelve to eighteen months.

It is curious that with the red wines this process of giving them fizziness seems to rob them of any subtlety of taste such as you will find in even ordinary still burgundy. The final effect is acceptable but uninteresting. White sparkling burgundy, on the other hand, I consider much more agreeable. Even the best brands lack the finesse of champagne, but as long as they are not too sweet they make pleasant aperitifs and go well at unsophisticated parties. The richness of burgundy gives a generous body to this wine, and I genuinely enjoyed it as an aperitif served, with proper local patriotism, before one of the dinners of the *Confrérie du Tastevin*.

Sparkling white burgundy is not a substitute for champagne, but an agreeable and economical alternative.

The process was started at Nuits-St-Georges early in the nineteenth century, and now it has spread to Beaune, Chablis, Chagny, Mercurey, Meursault, Pommard, Rully and Savigny. There are also members of the duly constituted *Syndicat des Producteurs de Vins Mousseux Méthode Champenoise de Bourgogne* in the towns of Mâcon and Tournus.

The well-known shippers Patriarche, of Beaune, introduced, shortly before I wrote this, an inexpensive sparkling wine called Kriter. This does not claim to be made by the *méthode champenoise*, but has adopted an accelerated German process, and does not guarantee any specific period in bottle before shipment. However the result is quite acceptable if the wine is sold on its own merits.

There are sparkling burgundies whose secondary fermentation has been effected in a tank, and not in a bottle. This can be admitted, if not approved. Beware, however, of brands (which can be called sparkling burgundy in Great Britain, though not in France) in which the sparkle has been achieved, not by a secondary fermentation but by the addition of carbon dioxide. There are also on our market so-called sparkling burgundies made in Burgundy but with percentages of the grapes coming from the Loire, the Rhône, etc. They are quite decent, pure drinks, but not burgundies.

Some of the sparkling red burgundy is so light in colour – through the short contact of the juice with the skins – that it is really sparkling *rosé*. This is very pretty to look at in the glass, but rather thin in taste.

Good still *rosés*, however, are made on a fairly large scale in Burgundy. Nuits-St-Georges is the capital of this trade, but you find it also in the Mâconnais. They vinify their wine in this way when it threatens to be too harsh as a red. This Mâconnais *rosé* is at any rate free from the cloying tendencies of, e.g., some of the Loire wines of this nature. There is *rosé* from the Beaujolais too, and some of this is vinified *en gris* by means of an even quicker separation of the juice from the skins. This 'grey' wine tastes quite well as a longish drink on a hot day if consumed near to where it was made, but it is a true example of wine that does not travel. (This inability to travel is often used, I think, by merchants as an excuse for not stocking wines for which there is a limited demand. Most wines that have a sufficient alcoholic strength will travel.)

My favourite Burgundian *rosé* is that of Marsannay, where the *Cave Coopérative des Grands Vins Rosés de Marsannay* is well known. Marsannay was once reputed for its reds. Then, on account of the growth of Dijon and the increasing local demand for inexpensive wine, most of the fields were turned over in the nineteenth century from *pinot* to *gamay*. But recently they have started growing the *pinot* again for their *rosé*, which they make properly, and not by the easy expedient of mixing red wine with white.

The *rosé* de Marsannay is quite dry, and a glass or two of this taken as an aperitif in the pretty courtyard of the Restaurant des Gourmets (M. Gauthier) on the edge of the village makes an enjoyable prelude to the succulent meals served there – for which there is also an excellent list of more serious burgundies for table wines. Georges Rozet speaks of these *rosés* de Marsannay as having a *gentille frivolité* which ends the Côte de Nuits (if you are working it northwards) with a kind of *gavotte digestive*.

The word 'digestive' suggests spirits. Burgundy makes these too.

Most of the makers of burgundy keep the skins, pips and stalks for a month or two after the pressing of the wine, and then have this pulp distilled into marc. A certain delay before distillation improves the quality of the brandy into which it is to be turned, but the must (*gennes* is the local name) has to be very carefully sealed meanwhile and kept from the air. During the winter mobile stills travel the various *communes*, distillation is effected under the supervision of government inspectors (private stills are forbidden), and the product is then called Eau-de-vie-de-Marc-de Bourgogne, which is usually abbreviated to Marc de Bourgogne. The c in marc is not pronounced, but the r is given a kind of nasal rolling effect with an element of an h sound in it.

The maximum alcoholic strength reached is 71°, but it is usually about 50° as it comes from the still. This must be reduced before sale to 40°. The marc should be matured in oak casks, whose tannin gives colour to the liquor. If really well-matured it is an admissible if not particularly commendable *eau de vie*. The marc of the Hospices de Beaune is an example, as is that of Louis Latour, which is a really superior version of this spirit. Some of the young stuff, however, though it may make a life-saving tot for the *vigneron* during a long winter day's work in the vineyard, tastes pretty raw on the palate of an effete amateur. I have had some marc – particularly in Chablis – whose taste recalled, over the many years, the smell of the acetylene lamps that were used in the early days of motoring.

Even rarer in the export trade, but a much better drink, is the Fine Bourguignonne, or Eau-de-vie de Vin de Bourgogne. This, as the latter name implies, is made from the distillation of *wine*, as in cognac and armagnac. But by a curious paradox good wine does not make good brandy (have you ever tried the wine of the Charente, from which cognac is made, as a table wine?), and perhaps burgundy is too good. In any event there is too much demand for burgundy as wine to make it commercially reasonable to distil it and turn it into brandy. However, some of the shippers do this on a small scale for their own tables and their friends', maturing it patiently through long years in cask, and I really enjoyed it recently at the end of a meal offered by Robert Drouhin, after the full, generous fare of Burgundian hospitality.

Cassis is a liqueur of from 15° to 20° alcohol made of black-currant juice, much used in Burgundy as a digestive or else combined with a sharp young *aligoté* as an aperitif. For the latter purpose the proportion should be one of cassis to three of wine. I am not much of a man for mixed drinks, but I think this is a good one. It is worthwhile to keep a bottle of cassis on hand for making summer aperitifs.

In Burgundy this drink is known as *un Kir*. It is named after Canon Félix Kir, a remarkable priest who died in his ninety-third year and who until near the end of his life was both mayor of Dijon and the city's representative in the *Chambre des Députés*. He was a tiny man with a great spirit, and had a memorable resistance record during the German occupation of the Second War. He was in the death-cell for two months, after having been caught in helping prisoners of the Germans to escape, and after the Liberation he was miraculously saved from the bullet of a collaborator by a thick wallet. *Vin blanc cassis* was his favourite aperitif, and for me the thought of this makes *un Kir* the more enjoyable.

Cassis can also be mixed with ice and water or soda for a dashing long drink for youngsters.

Crème de cassis is a sweeter version of cassis, to be used as a liqueur only, for those who like a sweet digestive. It is not good in *vin blanc* cassis. Prunelle de Bourgogne, made from sloes, is another Burgundian liqueur, of about 40°, which has a distinctive taste and gives pleasure to a large body of consumers. Of whom, rightly or wrongly, I am not one.

14. The New Vinification -- or the Old?

Recently there has been much controversy among burgundy-lovers about the vinification of their favourite wine, with comparisons of the results of the so-called *méthode nouvelle* and the *méthode ancienne*.

Now in a book written by an amateur for amateurs (and you can italicize the word amateur/s or not, as you prefer), the less said about details of vinification the better. This is too technical a subject to be gone into by anyone but a professional. It should be left to oenologists and vintners.

However, though I have no intention of describing, step by step, the various processes, the arguments about the two systems have been too widespread, and perhaps too heated, for me to ignore them altogether. The end-product, the wine, is very much a matter of interest to the drinker.

In general terms, the *méthode ancienne* may be said to have consisted of only partial removal of the stalks from the grapes of red wine (*égrappage partiel*) before they were put into the fermenting vats, and of leaving the must in contact with the grape-skins for a considerable period, up to sixteen or even twenty days. This prolonged vinification filled the wine with a considerable body of tannin, and meant consequently that it would take long to mature. So it could not be bottled for at least two years, and often not for four. But it would correspondingly live longer before fading.

The *méthode nouvelle* involves complete de-stemming (*égrappage total*), or almost complete, for red wines, a short period of contact between the must and the skins, perhaps even as little as four days, and therefore an accelerated vinification. Bottling of such wine can be effected soon after the wine reaches a year of age, and it can be consumed with pleasure correspondingly early. But the wines fade sooner.

That great authority, Harry Waugh, wrote in *Wine* magazine, 'In Burgundy, since 1947, they have been leaving the must on the skins for a much shorter period after fermentation, and the wines that have been aimed at and produced latterly are light in colour and lighter in body, much better *commercially* [my italics], but they have not kept so well. Now there are certain people who have kept to the *méthode ancienne*, or they are going back to it. That means keeping the skins with the must for about seventeen days after the actual fermentation.'

Early in the debate M. Louis Latour, who is one of the best *domaine*-bottlers and shippers, and a champion of reasonably quick vinification, intervened to claim that the epithets *ancienne* and *nouvelle* were misleading, as quick vinification was habitual until near the end of the nineteenth century, and that the so-called *méthode ancienne* prevailed only in the half century before the Second World War. Now I have not been able to trace any reference to *égrappage total* in old histories of burgundy, but certainly the vinification seems to have been comparatively swift in the eighteenth and early nineteenth centuries. Perhaps therefore it would be safer to avoid invidious epithets (to some people anything *ancien* is desirable, anything *nouveau* deplorable, and with others vice versa) and to refer only to delayed or accelerated vinification.

Now whenever delayed vinification was introduced, what is certain is that there was a change of method after the end of the Second World War. Dealers found themselves short of stocks and faced with an enormous demand released both at home and overseas by the reopening of communications. In this crisis it seemed impossible to continue making red wine that would need up to four years before it could be bottled and, say, eight before it could be enjoyed. Advantage was taken of improved means of scientific control of fermentation, to accelerate the making of red wine. The resultant wine was, as I have indicated, freer of tannin, softer, sooner ready for bottling, and therefore for the table. As to a shorter prospective life, how many people now try to keep wines to a great age?

It was claimed, naturally, that these changes were in accord with contemporary taste – that the new generation of drinkers preferred the younger, softer wines. I must admit that I am always somewhat sceptical about arguments concerning consumers' enthusiasm for changes that primarily suit the producers. But it must be allowed that there is a similar tendency, if not so marked, to accelerate vinification in Bordeaux also.

Again in *Wine* magazine, M. Robert Drouhin, another famous *domaine*-bottler and shipper, added his contribution to the debate. He pointed out that formerly the *pinot noir* grapes were small, and a considerable number of them were badly formed. The wines vinified in the 'traditional' way were full of tannin and usually hard. In order to sell the vintages younger, he explained, the vinification had been speeded up, and the wines became softer and sooner ready. However he added that in the last few years new methods of viticulture had produced larger berries of greater uniformity. These give a naturally softer wine, even with prolonged vinification, so that a number of vintners were going back to the slower method.

At his *domaine*, he said, the stalks were no longer completely removed from the bunches, the vatting was carried out in the old way with a head of skins floating on the top, and wine was left in the vat for eight to ten days for fermentation, which is twelve to thirteen days from the pressing. The result is, for fine *crus*, soft wines which are soon ready but can still be kept for a long time – though he added that this method would not be suitable for lesser wines like Côte de Beaune Villages.

M. René Engel is famous both as an oenologist and a wine-maker. When I talked with him at his house at Vosne-Romanée he took a middle view. ('Fools rush in where Engel fears to tread.') He said that he believed in prolonged vini-fication for fine *crus*, but that *commune* and lesser wines are suitable for quick vinification and early bottling and sale.

M. Aubert de Vilaine, of the Domaine de la Romanée-Conti, is of course concerned with fine wines only. He told me that good *cuvées* should be given the longest possible fermentation, and in years when there is a natural deficiency of tannin the *domaine* uses almost no *égrappage*. In the unhappy year 1965 they used none at all.

Yet another famous shipper, M. Doudet-Naudin, spoke out as an uncompromising champion of prolonged vinifica-tion. A good critic has said that his wines remind one of what burgundy used to taste like between the wars. His Beaune Clos du Roi seems to have much more body than most contemporary beaunes, even of superior *crus*.

With beaujolais, I was told by a leading shipper, M. Jean Thorin jr, *égrappage total* of *gamays* is likely to lead to a flabby wine. Some stems must be left in the vats to provide what they call *charpenterie* – a graphic word indicating the structure and body of the wine.

I suppose, as often, the best general solution is compromise. Every *cuvage* is a different entity, each *cru* and year requires special handling, and for settling such problems scientific guidance is now available where before the vintner had to depend on his experience and flair. It seemed to me during my investigations in Burgundy that most of the shippers fol-low a halfway course, practising almost but not quite total *égrappage* for *pinots*, and leaving the must in contact with the skins an average of eight days. With *gamays*, total *égrappage* is not desirable. In any case, great care is always observed in the pressing, so that the pips are not crushed; otherwise a woody taste is imparted to the wine, which some people mistake for corkiness. But a corked wine is undrinkable, whereas a woody wine is not definitely unpleasant and in fact is rather liked by some winemen.

With this middle method for the vinification of red burgundies and with early bottling, as soon as the wine has established its character, the wine becomes agreeable early, but still has some lasting quality – certainly up to ten years for the Côte d'Or, perhaps six years for beaujolais (longer for Moulin-à-Vent). Such wine, which has finesse and elegance though no great staying power, probably does best suit the needs of the average drinker. But for the old-fashioned amateur, who likes more colour and weight in his burgundy, there is always the possibility of getting such bottles with the help of an intelligent merchant, from shippers who have continued vinifying in the pre-war style, or at any rate have gone back to it.

M. de Courcel, then French ambassador to the Court of St James, said at the Vintners' Hall in 1967, 'The French drink French wines too early, the English drink them too late.' *Chacun à son gout.* In any case, M. le Comte de Moucheron told me, burgundy should be bottled as soon as possible, whenever it was to be drunk. He sees no point in keeping wine in the wood after it has formed its character. M. Philippe Marion, the technical director of Calvet, favours bottling red Côte de Beaune in fifteen to twenty months, and Côte de Nuits not much later. Certainly I have greatly enjoyed some Vosne-Romanées that were fully vinified and bottled early. The result was a most attractive fruitiness, combined with innate rounded strength.

All of the foregoing refers to red wine, as has been indicated from time to time in the text. The process for white burgundy is quite different, and not disputed. As I am not writing a textbook it is unnecessary to describe this, but all agree that *chardonnays* and *aligotés* must be fully *égrappés*, and the juice removed rapidly from the skins. Fermentation takes place in the casks, not in the vats. The higher alcoholic content of the whites frees them from the trouble in cask that the reds often suffer, with a kind of change of life, not once as with humans, but three times a year at the three critical seasons for the vines – at their sprouting, their flowering and their collection. These changes call for much care and skill on the part of the shippers, and to some considerable extent explain the widely different reputations that they have acquired.

White burgundy can be successfully made in small quantities, whereas red burgundy must be made in substantial quantities in large *cuves*.

This leads to the question of the effect of the introduction of the vast new tanks, enamel- or glass-lined, which are now so commonly used. I discussed these with several shippers. The general opinion is that they do not hurt ordinary wines; indeed, these may be helped by their bulk storage, as the wine in a magnum is usually better than that in a bottle, and in a bottle better than in a half-bottle. But the consensus is that fine wines must be matured in oak, and there is much concern about the dearth of young coopers to maintain the quality of the barrels when the present generation has passed away.

Finally, regarding the somewhat academic debate concerning the merits of burgundy today in comparison with the inter-war period, M. de Moucheron drew an illuminating analogy. Through preventive medicine, he said, and improved hygiene, more men live to a great age now than previously, but the average old man of today is not as hearty as the exceptional old man of the past who had the constitution to survive the perils of his epoch. So today, thanks to the aid of science, there is much more good burgundy than of yore, though the finest wines may not be as great as the rarer supreme bottlings of the past. To which, however, I should append another dictum of M. René Engel – that the aid of chemistry should be invoked only for the vines, not for the wines. Doctored wines always betray their artificiality to the expert.

15. 'Generic' Burgundy – or Authentic?

Another current controversy is concerned with the incorrect use of Burgundian *appellations* on the labels of bottles whose contents bear little or no relationship to their supposed places of origin.

My fellow wine-writers and I had for some time been warning our specialized audiences against such practices, particularly in the cases of beaujolais, chablis and certain *communes* of the Côte d'Or such as Nuits-St-Georges, Beaune and Pommard. Then in December 1966 the *Sunday Times* brought these anomalies to the attention of a wider public – though in fact they had been anticipated, as regards beaujolais, by the *Sunday Mirror* and, curiously, by a magazine known under the comprehensive title of *Competitors' Journal & Money Matters*.

It is unnecessary to parade all the detailed statistics to prove the point. They can be summed up by the *Sunday Times*'s comparison of the official French figures showing that 600,000 gallons of what may legitimately be called burgundy were exported to England in 1965 with the estimate of the Wine & Spirit Association of Great Britain that we annually consume at least $2\frac{1}{2}$ million gallons of this (*sic*) wine.

For the victims of the cruder forms of such misrepresentation I have little sympathy. A man who goes for 15% interest on deposits should not be surprised if the 'bank' fails. A man who buys motor insurance at about half the rates of the tariff companies must be prepared suddenly to find himself without cover. So with the purchaser of a vintage 'Nuits-St-Georges' in Soho for 60p a bottle. It will taste like a *gros vin* of the Midi or of Algeria – precisely because it is a *gros vin* of the Midi or

Algeria. Possibly he will not know the difference. But he may decide, not unreasonably, that he does not think much of burgundy.

Such frauds, however, are not confined to the wine trade. Human cupidity and credulity being what they are, only a myriad horde of government inspectors could eradicate all commercial mendacity, and this remedy would be worse than the disease. The old rule of *caveat emptor* is the simplest protection for the consumer. A buyer who exercises no caution should not complain if he is deceived.

But leaving aside the grosser falsifications of a minority, what was really serious in the aftermath of these newspaper revelations was the admission by several apparently respectable wine-chains, and even some independent merchants, of their practice of blending minor burgundies (with perhaps some tolerable but cheaper ingredients from elsewhere) and selling them under the name of well-known controlled *appellations*. And they even tried to justify this.

They claimed to be judges of what the public expected of the name of Pommard, for instance, and to be performing a service by blending wines – say some Arrière-Côtes de Beaune with a touch of Côtes du Rhône – to accord with such expectations. Otherwise, they said, purchasers would be 'confused' – which seemed to me a rather disingenuous use of the word. I should have thought it would have been less confusing to sell them real Pommard.

Unconvincing arguments were put forward about Dundee cakes not having to be made in Dundee, and about a Cornish pasty representing a recipe, not a regional dish. Similarly certain wine-names, they said, are 'generic', not geographic. Volnay, for instance, is a type, not a place.

They also asserted that, by these means, they were keeping down the cost of 'burgundy'. It is true that they have kept down the cost, but personally I do not greatly appreciate the bargain if I save money by not getting what I want.

Not that this practice is confined to burgundy. How many little Palus and/or Bourg wines reach the market as Médoc, or even as St-Julien? But even more exotic mixtures seem to enter our cheaper claret. Observers have reported fleets of Portuguese wine-tankers steaming up the Gironde to unload at Bordeaux. Perhaps they were all carrying *porto* for aperitifs, as it is an offence in France to mix foreign wine with French.

Nor do I believe that the substitutions of burgundy are confined to Great Britain. I do not claim to know what is going on in the trades of other countries, but I have had some very curious bottles of alleged Côte d'Or wines in Holland and the United States – which is perhaps the reason, of which I have already spoken, for discriminating Americans insisting on *domaine*-bottled or single-vineyard burgundies. Even in France, outside Burgundy (where they know too much to accept this), I have been served with very unconvincing *commune* burgundies.

However, we in Britain did lay ourselves open to French criticism by refusing to have anything to do with their *AC* regulations. Eventually, I suppose, we shall have to do so, now we are in the Common Market. Meanwhile the *AC* laws themselves operate to facilitate misrepresentation so long as French shippers are allowed to export *AC* wines without the corresponding *acquits* and *titres* – permits and way-bills, as one might say.

It is unnecessary to go into all the anomalous situations that the rules still permit. They have been described by various authorities, such as Dermot Morrah in *Wine & Food*, Julian Jeffs in *Focus*, Edmund Penning-Rowsell in *Vintage* and Phillip Cook in *Ridley's Wine and Spirit Trade Circular*. It will be enough to quote a single example of what may have happened.

Say a shipper in Burgundy has the right to sell 100 hogsheads of a given *AC* wine. A British importer buys ten. He is not interested in the *AC* labels. Indeed, by disclaiming them he gets the wine at a lower price than would be asked with them. What does the French shipper do with the corresponding *AC* permits for these ten hogsheads? Does he return them to the *AC* officials, or destroy them? May they not somehow get attached to other bottles? . . . And there are other possibilities of evasion.

The *AC* regulations are theoretically admirable, but they invoke a mass of paper-work. (*Paperasserie* is the descriptive French word.) Anyone who has served in the armed forces knows how much fiddling can be practised with forms.

There are at least 250 shippers in Burgundy and, as the statistics in Chapter 2 have shown, nearly 100,000 different makers of wine. They are splendid types, these Burgundians, but by the mere law of averages not all can be completely incorruptible. Some burgundy, I am sure, is loaded in its home country with Rhône wine, if no worse; some, I have even presumed to think, is touched up with brandy. If such mistakes occur, can we be sure of the observation of absolute legality in the use of *AC* labels?

No, the French wine trade, from the original grower to the ultimate retailer, varies in its degrees of commercial integrity just as does any wine trade elsewhere – or any trade, for that matter.

Even the most scrupulous supplier has no control over the wine after it reaches the *hôtelier* or *restaurateur*. Here frequently titles get changed and plebeian wine becomes ennobled. There was the cartoon of the hotel cellar-man filling bottles marked with different labels, according to the orders received from the tables, out of the same barrel. And the joke about the *maître d'hôtel* saying to the *sommelier*, 'We're overstocked with '52s, change half of them to '53.' True? Or false? Perhaps exaggerated. Certainly in France there is the well-intentioned *Service de Répression des Fraudes* in the background, as a threat to such dishonesty. But it is well known that this service is parlously understaffed. In this country, except for the Customs (who are most meticulous), the authorities seem little interested in wine. I was a magistrate for many years and heard numerous cases concerning adulteration of food, milk and even beer. But never a single prosecution about wine. In any restaurant the bottle should of course be presented for inspection before it is opened.

However I must come back to our 'generic' Beaunes and Nuits-St-Georges. Here we have our wine trade not merely admitting their existence, but seeking to justify them. Certainly there was always much opposition to this within their ranks, but the purists were for long out-voted in the councils of the representative association of the trade. This embraces a multiplicity of interests, from huge brewing and distilling concerns, through wholesalers and retail chains, to the few remaining independent merchants. Even under the stress of the revelations by the *Sunday Times* this disparate body appeared reluctant to reform and certainly slow to take action. Naturally, long-standing trade practices, however misguided, cannot be abolished overnight. But I should have welcomed a greater show of desire to put them right with all possible alacrity.

The trade has warned us that when things are cleaned up – by an acceptance of *AC* rules (suitably modified for a consuming, not a producing, country) or by other means – we shall have to pay more for our burgundies. So be it. I started by saying that good burgundy is an expensive drink. But if I cannot afford a genuine Nuits-St-Georges I can buy a *bourgogne*, a *bourgogne grand ordinaire*, or even a *passe-tout-grains*. At least I shall know what I am getting.

We are also told that such a reform will lead to the extension of the sale of blended wines under branded names. This extension has already set in, anyhow. And a blended wine under a branded name is preferable to a blended wine under an *AC* name.

There is, in fact, nothing wrong with branded wines. After all, sherries and champagnes fall into this category. Even for table wines, these form the staple drink of the majority of customers in some of the great wine-producing countries of the world. They can be quite good, and quite good value. To me personally they are rather uninteresting. A branded wine is like an unexceptional White Paper composed by a committee, rather than a book written by a single author. The book may be good, bad or indifferent, but it at least will have some seal of individuality. However, I grant that branded wines are perfectly satisfactory to most consumers, for most purposes. And for the gala occasion they can rise to the authentic bottle of the *commune*, if not even of the vineyard.

These 'generic' Beaunes, etc., that have been in too common distribution have not been bad wines, nor, at their prices, bad value. In fact they have often been quite good, and reasonably priced. They just have not been the real thing. They have misled the public, and retarded the development of their taste for the variable but genuine burgundy.

Until all these anomalies are cleared up by the EEC, the man in the better street may ask how he can be sure of getting genuine bottles. Well, reform in the trade's use of names is already under way, and may well be becoming effective by the time this book is re-published. Meanwhile, however, for the level of taste of people who might read it, realism is necessary about prices, and care about sources.

As I write I have been looking at the current price-lists of a dozen London merchants. As a result of this survey I should not feel secure that I was buying the right thing from them if I were paying less than £1·25 retail for a bottle of Côte d'Or *commune*, ready for drinking, or less than £1·50 for a superior *commune* of a good year. Single-vineyard wines from fine fields come at £1·75 upwards – and quite some way upwards for *grands crus* or Hospices *cuvées*. For *domaine* bottling, or even just French bottling, I should have to pay appreciably more, which I should not think worth while for *commune* wines. These prices are before VAT.

But for the diligent seeker there are still considerable rewards. An occasional single-vineyard wine from an unfashionable *commune* seems to offer extraordinary value. For instance, a reliable shipper, in November 1972, quoted Fixin Clos Napoléon '69 at only £1·15; and I found three merchants offering the leading 1st *cru* of Santenay, Les Gravières, at from £1 to £1·35; two of '67, a goodish year, and one of '64, a good year – the last for laying down. Admittedly Santenay is right at the end of the Côte d'Or, but it still is in the Côte d'Or, and my somewhat unenthusiastic comment on it on page 103 referred to its *commune* wines rather than its 1st *crus*.

These prices are from the most recent catalogues. I cannot foresee what inflation may have done to them even before this book is published. Perhaps some day we shall have another Chancellor of the Exchequer like Gladstone, who will promote health and happiness by decreasing the tax on table wines . . .

Meanwhile, since these prices are too high for daily drinking, there remain the pleasing minor blends like Vins Fins de la Côte de Nuits or Côtes de Beaune; there remain the mâconnais and beaujolais bottles, at appreciably less than the figures quoted above. There are still, too, *bourgogne* and *bourgogne grand ordinaire* or *bourgogne ordinaire* already referred to. (Perhaps I should repeat that *bourgogne* is better than *bourgogne grand ordinaire*, and that there is only a difference of name between the latter and *bourgogne ordinaire*.)

If you know the right merchant you can find excellent stuff under the modest category of *bourgogne*. Much of this (as I said in Chapter 4) is 'declassified' *commune* or even single-vineyard wine which has been made in excess of the *AC* limits of the *commune* or single-vineyard yield, and can only be sold under the comprehensive humble name.

But – 'If you know the right merchant' . . . How do you find him? We still have a number of independents who know and love their burgundy, and will be glad to guide anyone who does not yet entirely trust his own palate, but shows genuine interest. Even those 'wicked' brewers and distillers, though principally interested in turnover and return on capital, have had the sense not to take away all individuality of buying from the famous retailers whom they now control.

When, many years ago, I started to drink burgundy, one could buy a good single-vineyard wine for about 48s. a case. (True, 48s. meant more then than it does now, but on the other hand taxes took much less of one's income, and left more disposable. To do the shippers and merchants justice, taxation now forms a much higher proportion of the price than it did then. They have been very reasonable in their own increases.) So there was not much point in buying *commune* wines. Anyhow, before the *Institut National des Appellations d'Origine des Vins* (*INAO* as it is called) was formed, these were admittedly pretty unreliable in Burgundy itself, apart from any alterations made in England.

However, in London when I was young there were at least a couple of dozen entirely trustworthy merchants from whom one could get disinterested guidance; and one at least in most important provincial centres. Later, when economic stringency hit us after the Second World War and single-vineyard wines became treats for high feasts, I admit I was somewhat puzzled by some of the *commune* wines to which I had descended. I now know why. They were our friends the 'generics'.

Meanwhile other sources of advice had become available. André Simon, the great mentor of my generation, had founded the Wine & Food Society and started publishing its invaluable journal *Wine & Food*. Non-technical books on wine began to appear, at first a trickle but now a spate. Wine articles by qualified critics appear in several magazines, and those in some newspapers are reliable. Wine has become a subject of conversation outside the esoteric circles of connoisseurs. Talk among fellow wine-lovers, with its generous exchange of experience, is the best means of evaluating shippers – a most important point in connection with burgundy. No man can know all the shippers by himself. Incidentally some of the famous shippers of my youth and middle age have not retained the reputations they then had. Lapses of generations, and even complete changes of control, have altered the table of merit.

So even while 'generic' names still survive, and the demand for burgundy remains four times the supply, it is still perfectly possible for the prudent and interested buyer to get unimpeachable *appellations*. He must read the authorities, choose his merchant carefully and familiarize himself, by test or on advice, with the shippers whose products are the most reliable. He must be prepared to pay a fair price, and if he cannot afford the fair price of a really good wine he should content himself with modest but genuine *petits vins*, rather than buy the name, but not the reality, of something better.

At times I think wine-critics become a little too captious. A single bad bottle should not necessarily damn a merchant, a shipper or a vineyard. How often does one get a tough steak or a tasteless cheese! But wine, which has innumerable processes of preparation and a much longer period of risk before it comes to the table, is subject to many more vicissitudes than other foods, and allowance should be made accordingly.

I was recently asked to arbitrate about a bottle of Aloxe-Corton of a good year, from a well-known shipper – though not one whose products I greatly admire. It was certainly very bad stuff. So bad, in fact, that I am sure something had happened to it after it was shipped.

A definitely corked bottle, of course, will always be replaced, but in my experience these are quite rare. Troubles that develop in the cask should be eliminated before bottling, but there are still mishaps – principally through variations in temperature – that can occur in shipping or cellaring. Some shippers too now seem to me to take much of the life out of their wines by excessive filtering, to get an unnaturally bright colour.

There is something to be said for occasionally drinking bad wine. It is illuminating, if only by contrast. A tycoon who only drinks peerless bottles (if there be such a person) can never get to appreciate their real virtues.

Sound corks, of ample length, are most important. Petty economy in corks damns a shipper in my eyes. I also have a personal phobia, probably quite irrational, for the use of plastic in place of lead-foil for capsules.

I have endorsed the growing practice of early bottling of burgundy, but I have run into trouble with beaujolais (most of which you want to drink young) because it had been too recently bottled. The wine, except for beaujolais *nouveau*, needs two or three months to settle down in its new container. I have learned from this experience to inquire when a wine was bottled, if I plan to drink it soon.

Ultimately your own palate must be the judge. (It is, so to speak, the *palais de justice*.) With experience, fortified by discussion (which is the best aid to memory) and reading, any interested person who is not suffering from some abnormality of taste or smell can develop a reasonable comparative judgement on wine. Few faculties can provide greater enjoyment.

The very difficulties of burgundy – its northern situation, with the consequent over-chaptalization: its hazards of frost and hail, exaggerating the variations of the vintages: the past and, we hope, passing misuse of its place names – make it the more interesting test of your taste. And when you know enough to get well-made wines, even of some quite modest provenance, all your disappointments seem rewarded. As a final assurance – though the premium is rather costly – you can buy *domaine*-bottled or single-vineyard wines, and equalize the cost by drinking decent little growths in the intervals between such festivities.

16. Burgundian Food

It is a commonplace that good wine areas, at any rate in Europe, tend to produce good food also. The cuisine goes with the cellar. Palates trained to appreciate good wine reject bad cooking. And it would be natural that the style of the wine should influence the character of the dishes.

It certainly does so in Burgundy. The full, robust wines call for rich, flavoursome *plats* to accompany them.

Fortunately Burgundy is well endowed, in its forests, streams and pastures, with material for the kitchen. There is abundant game, excellent fish (though somewhat limited in variety) and splendid cattle, as befits the home of the great Charollais beef breed (Charolles is a village of Burgundy). Its poultry approaches the distinction of the nearby Bresse. The *charcuterie* is varied and full-flavoured. There are numerous local cheeses of merit. Dijon mustard is the most famous of France, and congenial at any rate to the more modest growths of Burgundian wine; indeed it is based on wine. They raise here the tenderest snails, I think, in the whole country – perhaps because these feed on vine-leaves. Alligny in the Morvan claims the somewhat specialized honour of producing the best turnips in the world. Round the edges of the woods mushrooms, truffles and *morilles* thrive. The local *feuilleté aux morilles* is particularly appetizing.

The diet of Burgundy is appetizingly depicted in Colette's stories of her girlhood – its simple ingredients patiently prepared with housewifely skill, recalling the best of provincial life in a traditional France that threatens to pass away. The ideal has been described as *des plats bien cuisinés et des vins qui ne le sont pas*; *cuisine*, it will be remembered, is an opprobrious term in wine-making, as we say of accounts that they have been 'cooked'.

There are half a dozen or more famous dishes allied to Burgundian names, beginning with *boeuf bourguignonne*, *oeufs bourguignonne* (poached in red wine and served on *croûtons*), *coq au Chambertin*, *poulet poché Chablisienne*, *potée bourguignonne*, *jambon persillé de Bourgogne*, *terrine bourguignonne*, *filets de sole Nicolas Rolin*, and so on.

The *terrine bourguignonne* is compounded of pork, veal, shallots, parsley, bay leaf and chablis, packed in truffled strips of bacon. The *potée bourguignonne*, one of the most characteristic of local dishes, consists of shoulder of ham, chine of pork, bacon and sausages, cooked in a soup tureen with cloves, leeks, carrots and *bouquet garni*. Then cabbages and new potatoes are added, and the whole turned out on a plate with rows of vegetables alternating with meat. So simple, yet so painstakingly made, and so delicious.

The *pouchouse* is another famous regional dish. The classic recipe calls for four fish of the Saône – pike, perch, tench and eels, but other fish are used as available – simmered in a dry white wine of the Côte de Beaune and cream, with cloves of garlic cooked till dissolved. It is traditionally accompanied by Meursault. A similar dish cooked in red wine is called a *matelote*.

The *quenelles de brochet* have already been mentioned. The laborious pounding and sieving of this coarse fish, poached and flaked, gives it an incredible lightness and delicacy – though perhaps it appears too often in the *menus touristiques* of the restaurants in these days. It can be accompanied by a cream sauce or, more often, by one made of the local crayfish. The streams and lakes are full of these crayfish; they go admirably with all white wine, but particularly with chablis. *Meurette* is a Burgundian stew of eels cooked in wine, red or white to taste.

The *charcuterie* is copious and varied. There are wild boar in the forest of the Morvan, whence also comes the delicious *jambon de Morvan à la crème*, and its smoked raw ham is one of the best of France. *Boudins, andouillettes, cervelas* and all other kinds of savoury sausages are offered in profusion; most are served hot, particularly in the Mâconnais. The banquets of the *Confrérie du Tastevin* traditionally begin with sucking pig *en gelée* and the local *jambon persillé*, carried in procession to musical honours. *Jambon à la lie de vin* is another local speciality. Most Burgundians season such dishes liberally with Dijon mustard.

All kinds of *pâtés* and *terrines* are made of the multifarious game of the region, and enough rabbits seem to have escaped the myxomatosis to provide inexhaustible *terrines de lapin*, usually served hot. Many of these *pâtés* and terrines are done *en croûte*. And there are *oreillons de veau farcis*, calves' ears stuffed with pounded pike and cooked in *aligoté*, which – rightly or wrongly – I cannot claim to have tried.

I have said that there are 400 different French cheeses exhibited at the Dijon gastronomic fair. Burgundy makes a good contribution. Chaource, Epoisses and St Florentin are perhaps the best known, and Cîteaux, though mild, is thought to go peculiarly well with red burgundy. There are also Cabrion, usually wrapped in plane leaves, and the highly flavoured Soumaintrain, which is allied to St Florentin but with a coloured rind. Thoissey, Chevrotins de Mâcon, and Vézelay are goat cheeses. *Gougères*, a kind of *brioche* lightly flavoured with local cheese, are a delicious feature of Burgundian meals in place of ordinary rolls. For tea or occasional snacks Dijon makes a famous spiced honey-cake called *pain d'épices*.

The snails are plentiful and excellent – much better than those you get elsewhere, which are now mostly imported from behind the Iron Curtain. These latter have the consistency, if not of iron, of rubber; but the Burgundian snails are as soft as mushrooms, are rarely overloaded with

garlic, and absorb the flavour of the wine in which they are
cooked.

There are no special mysteries about the matching of
burgundy to food. The usual rules obtain. However, it may
be noted again that good white burgundies will accompany
hot white meats and poultry quite satisfactorily – as well,
almost, as the softer reds of the Côte de Beaune. The more
delicate whites like chablis should not be put up against a fish
with a rich sauce, such as *homard à l'américaine* or *thermidor*.
Any Burgundian red will go with red meats, but the Côte de
Beaune reds, except perhaps a fine Aloxe-Corton, are not
quite full enough for game, for which the great Côte de Nuits
cuvées make a magnificent complement. There are no natural
burgundies for the sweet course, and if you want a complete
Burgundian wine list you must finish with a *bourgogne blanc
mousseux*; but I prefer this as an aperitif.

Any burgundy goes well with cheese, and it does not follow
that the powerful wines of Gevrey-Chambertin and Morey-St-
Denis should call for highly seasoned cheeses. Indeed with these
last I should prefer a Mercurey or a big beaujolais such as
Moulin-à-Vent or Côte de Brouilly. Milder cheeses seem to
me more subtly to evoke the beauties of the great wines of
the Côte de Nuits. But fine red burgundies stand up to rich
sauces and spicy dishes better than clarets do.

All burgundies are good for cooking, though few of us can
now afford to use the fine *crus* in the kitchen. However Julian
Jeffs told me about a kind of blind tasting of two *coqs au vin*,
of which one was done in the traditional Chambertin and the
other in *bourgogne ordinaire*. No one was told which was
which. Everyone participating, layman or expert, preferred
the one cooked in Chambertin.

Elizabeth David's *French Provincial Cooking* has a good section on the old duchy, and Camille Rodier mentions three
books that have become local classics, namely Beaunois Contour's *Le Cuisinier Bourguignon*, Pierre Huguenin's *Meilleurs*

Recettes de ma Pauvre Mère, and Charles Blandin's *Cuisine et Chasse de Bourgogne et d'Ailleurs*.

Most Burgundian dishes are cooked with wine, cheese or cream, and some with all three, and there is much garnishing with pieces of salt pork, glazed onions and mushrooms, to form rich fare for people who work hard in all weathers in the open air. Poupon and Forgeot quote Curnonsky, 'the prince of gastronomes', as saying, 'By the glory of its vineyards, by the richness of its soil, by the excellence and quality of its natural products as well as the taste and talents of its chefs ... who for centuries have maintained the highest traditions, Burgundy has become a gastronomic paradise.' Alas, the rush of contemporary life, the intrusion of pre-prepared comestibles, the decline of consumers' standards, seem to me of recent years to have affected even the Burgundian cuisine. It is no longer possible to drop in on any little place and expect the perfect meal. One has to consult the stars in Michelin, and there is only one between Dijon and Beaune, though they come a little thicker in the Mâconnais and the Beaujolais. However, in the private homes, and particularly in those of the hospitable shippers, one still enjoys the most succulent Burgundian food accompanied by notable wine. Here, better perhaps than anywhere else, you will find preserved the best traditions of simple but rich French cooking passed down through generations that have really appreciated fine fare – and still do so.

17. The Care and Service of Burgundy

It is much more economical to buy burgundy young, as soon as you can evaluate its quality, than to wait and buy it when it is mature. Until you drink them, your bottles should be properly cellared, and those who lack facilities for this would be wise to pay their merchants the nominal sum they ask for storing clients' wine. This charge certainly does not equal the wine's appreciation in value.

You will not normally be drinking great *crus* on the spur of the moment; you will know in advance when they are needed, and can fetch them from the merchant at the appropriate time. But they need care in transport, and should be given a few days' rest before they are served. A really old bottle which may have thrown a heavy deposit is best decanted at the merchant's, well-stoppered, and taken home at most a few hours before the festive meal.

Ordinary burgundies keep well enough in a house or flat, providing their racks are in a quiet, dark, draught-free corner – as cool as possible, but the evenness of the temperature is more important than the degree.

I have spoken from time to time in the chapters devoted to specific areas about the age at which different kinds of burgundy should be consumed. However, even with the 'new' method of vinification there is no need to rush them, except beaujolais. More burgundy is currently drunk too early than too late. The new-style Côte d'Or wines still have an appreciable life, though they have not the twenty- and thirty-year staying power of the great *cuvées* of the past. A booklet called *Burgundy* by Erna Pinner, published by S. F. & O. Hallgarten, recalls that at a dinner given in Beaune in 1920, in honour of two Beaunois notables who had been awarded the *Légion d'Honneur* (not, after all, a very extraordinary distinction), the burgundies served were Montrachet 1858, Clos Vougeot blanc 1891, Romanée-St-Vivant 1898, La Tâche 1911, Richebourg 1876, Clos de Bèze 1870 and Musigny 1865. I very much doubt whether at a similar dinner in 2020 they will be serving burgundies dating back to 1958 (particularly white ones), and I am sure they will not feature the unhappy vintages of 1965 and 1968.

If one has to make rules about starting dates, I suggest keeping good Côte de Nuits wines at least six years; Côte de Beaune reds at least five, and its whites at least three (more if they are *grands crus*). Chablis *grands crus* need at least three years, 1st *crus* eighteen months, chablis and petit chablis a year. For chalonnais and mâconnais allow at least three for the reds, two for the whites; and drink beaujolais, except for Moulin-à-Vent and Côte de Brouilly, as soon as you like. The vins fins de la Côte de Nuits, Côte de Beaune Villages, *bourgogne*, *bourgogne grand ordinaire*, *passe-tout-grains* and *aligotés* are usually ready as soon as they are put on the market, but it may be helpful to repeat my suggestion of finding out when they were bottled and giving them at least two or three months after that. But all these are just minima, and you are more often rewarded than punished by restraint.

In applying such calculations it must be remembered that certain vintages mature very quickly, others are stubborn. The wine-magazines and the merchants keep us informed about such exceptions. The figures above are only averages.

Peter Reynier has an interesting theory that all burgundy has an attractive, fruity quality if drunk young, provided it has not been kept too long in the cask. (See Chapter 14 *re* early bottling.) Then, he says, it passes into a respectable but unexciting middle age, from which the finest bottles emerge, after long and careful cellaring, as incomparable masterpieces. This means they are rather like human beings, who are most interesting when young or old.

Now in current circumstances there is little risk of burgundy becoming too old, but I did keep my Beaune Clos-des-Mouches '52 red over long; the last bottles were agreeable, but a little tired. On the other hand, '55 was one of those abundant years that come on quickly and are supposed to be deficient in staying-power; but in the autumn of 1967 I had a Chambolle-Musigny '55 shipped by Lebègue-Bichot and bottled in London by Findlater, and it showed no vestige of decline. However, the man who has a case or two of a given *cru* and vintage which has reached maturity would be wise to test a bottle every few months, to make sure there is no premature decline.

It may have been noticed that, so far, I have only mentioned vintage years incidentally in this book. Vintage cards, such as those originated by the Wine & Food Society, have their uses for the layman when he is ordering in restaurants, but what the French call *le culte du millésime* can be overdone. No 'off' year is an entire failure in every vineyard, and (what is less generally recognized) no great year is equally successful everywhere. A percipient merchant can find good bottles for you from almost any vintage, and the unfashionable years provide gratifying economies for the purchaser. Therefore I have relegated the comparison of vintages to Appendix A. But in the meantime I shall add a personal note, that I have found that good proprietors and shippers make some enjoyable wine in every year. I expect to find even some of the aforementioned, currently despised 1968s quite acceptable.

So much for buying and keeping. Now for the service. Good red burgundy should be brought to the dining-room twenty-four hours in advance of the meal, and all red burgundy except beaujolais at least twelve hours – and stood upright. White wines can be brought straight from the bin to the refrigerator or ice-bucket, but it is best to give them six hours or so standing upright before chilling.

Burgundian authorities say that white burgundy should be served at from 6° to 10° centigrade, according to the weather (the warmer it is, the cooler should be the wine); and red burgundy (again other than the smaller beaujolais) at 15° to 16°. With the formula that everyone has at the tip of his tongue,

$$\text{Fahrenheit} = \frac{\text{Centigrade} \times 9}{5} + 32,$$

you will readily calculate on this basis that white wine should be from 43° to 50° Fahrenheit, and red 59° to 61° Fahrenheit. Because of the difficulty of judging the speed of the ice-bucket's effect I long ago gave up using one and found out how long to keep a bottle of, say, Meursault in my refrigerator; but like its owner, it is very old, and probably inefficient, so I shall not risk misleading the reader by giving the results of my experiments. Anyone can make his own calculations with his machine. Personally I think 43° rather cold for white wine, and likely to numb the flavour.

I hope it does not need to be said that red burgundy must reach about 60° naturally. If you have not brought it up soon enough, or if (horrid thought!) your dining-room does not reach that temperature, the only thing to do is to pour the wine as it is and warm it with your hands cupped round the glass. (As a precaution against such risks, wine glasses should be thin.) It is worse to serve a red burgundy too warm rather than too cold. On the other hand it is worse to serve a white burgundy too cold rather than cool.

Everyone agrees on the need of chambering red wines, but few join with me in my insistence on decanting them. I stand by the old adage, 'Good wine deserves decanting, poor wine needs it.' But I must admit that few Burgundians do this, and – even worse – that most of them serve their reds, fine old ones included, from those abominable wicker baskets which make it impossible to see when to stop pouring, and usually ensure that the lees will get into the last glass if indeed they are not distributed over all of them. It is significant that the French have no word for 'decanter'. The open-work wire cradles are at least less noxious than wicker ones, as they permit the host (or butler, if any nowadays) to judge when to stop pouring.

At a sociable lunch in London towards the end of 1966 I enjoyed a share in two magnums of Clos Vougeot '57, *mise du propriétaire* Joseph Drouhin, both of which had been opened at 12.15 for service about 2.15. As an experiment, one was decanted, the other just left uncorked. I must admit that the former tasted more like what I call a British burgundy, the latter more like a French one. That is to say, the decanted magnum seemed fuller, and perhaps even sweeter. The un-decanted one was lighter and fruitier. I suppose its comparative lack of oxygenation had kept the acids predominant over the sugars.

I was pleased however to note during a recent visit – as an offset against my dislike of the omni-present baskets – that the Burgundian *sommeliers* cut the entire lead-foil capsule right off the neck of the bottle, instead of just removing the circular top of it, as most British wine-waiters do. If a delicate wine runs over the lead-foil there is a risk of its absorbing the metallic taste.

It is unnecessary to go through the whole drill of opening, cleaning and decanting the bottle, as this is covered in every general wine-primer. But to return to decanting, I still think, with due respect to the Burgundians, that this old if passing British practice, probably coming from our training with port, is a good one, and that the consequent slight aeration of the wine improves it after its long imprisonment in the bottle. I can advance no scientific proof of this, but empirically I am convinced that it is so. Certainly the decanter should be one of the full-bellied types, which give the contents addi-tional aeration, and not some chic, 'modern', tall and narrow design. It is curious that air, which is so fatal to wine in its early youth, seems so helpful at the last hour.

If I have persuaded you of the justice of my decanting theory and you have a steady hand, you can pour the wine straight from the bottle into the decanter. In my own palsied age I have to use a funnel – of course one with a curved spout, so that the wine does not fall with a splash into the decanter, but slides gently down its flanks.

Candle-light is said by all the pundits to be the best for revealing the moment in decanting when the lees of an old wine start to move, and therefore when to stop pouring. But I have found that it is very difficult to get, and keep, the candle-flame to the right height. An electric torch, whose light you can fix, mounted on something so that the lens is opposite the neck of the bottle as you pour, is simpler to arrange and, in my experience, more efficient.

When to decant is a more difficult problem than whether to decant. It is impossible to be precise, for each bottle needs different treatment, but this can be pretty accurately estimated with experience. For a rough rule one might allow two hours before service for a young red wine, an hour for a youngish one, half an hour for a mature one, and a few minutes for a really old one. After decanting you can lay the stopper on, but not in, the neck of the decanter, to exclude an excess of oxygen, but then unless I am immersed in the social preliminaries of entertaining I try to remember to take the stopper off altogether about halfway through the period between decanting and the estimated moment of the service of the course which the wine is to accompany – which is usually reached later than you foresee. Not, it is to be noted, halfway between decanting and the beginning of the meal.

I find decanting is particularly helpful for youngish wines of a big year which have not fully absorbed their tannin.

Marcel Boulestin even taught me to decant white wines, and I still think they gain by this treatment, but this may be pushing a theory to extremes. Certainly, however, they look prettier in a clear decanter than in a darkish green bottle. In any case they must be decanted much later than red wines, in fact just after they have left the bucket or refrigerator, so that they will not lose their requisite chill.

If you do not decant you must at least de-cork red wines, to let them breathe; and my own experience is that they need more time for breathing in the bottle than they do in the decanter. This is natural, as they get less air in the bottle. Decanting obviously gives them a more complete aeration. Also I think that bottles that are not going to be decanted need rather longer to *chambrer* themselves than those which are to be eventually decanted.

Very occasionally a bottle of burgundy suffers from what is known as 'bottle-stench'. This is quite different from being corked. Corked wine will never be drinkable. But with decanting, and even with breathing, bottle-stench will soon pass away, and the wine will become agreeable. Decanting and, again, even breathing will also help a wine that is too woody, either from careless crushing of some pips in the press or from storage in a defective cask.

I hate those exaggeratedly large goblets, bigger even than brandy *ballons*, that they provide in some pretentious Burgundian restaurants, and also, it must be admitted, in some good ones, for even quite unimportant burgundies. (I was given one recently in Beaune for a young Savigny!) To drink from these you have to lie back in your chair, and risk dislocating your neck. A bottle split among six of such leaves only a faint smear in the bottom of each. But burgundy does call for a reasonably large glass, so that, when it is filled two-thirds full, you can twirl the wine round without spilling it. This rotation will release the volatile essences, even in quite unimportant wines, almost all of which have something for the nose, as well as bring out the voluptuous beauty of the *parfum* of the *grands crus*. Colourless, uncut glasses best reveal the loveliness of the colour of burgundy, from the pale green-gold glint of chablis to the magnificent crimson of the Gevrey-Chambertins.

It would not look very pretty at a mixed dinner, but at gatherings of *copains* assembled to discuss burgundy the wine can be rolled round in the mouth, while the drinker breathes in and out through the nose, in order to get the full savour. Another trick, to prolong the luscious after-taste of a fine burgundy, is to protrude your tongue through your closed lips when you have taken a sip. The relish of the wine then seems to go on re-echoing like distant thunder in a summer storm. This prolonged after-taste is one of the most amiable features of good burgundy.

They tell a story in Beaune of the guest of a famous gastronome, who had emptied his glass of a superb *cru* at one gulp. 'Sir,' said the host, 'when one has the honour to be invited to drink wine like this, one looks at it first, then one takes its bouquet, next one sips it, and finally one talks about it.' That talking about it is so important, particularly when one can discuss it with persons who know more about it than oneself (which has not been difficult to arrange in my own case). Well-informed opinion enormously increases one's appreciation of wine. It is based on an immense accumulated lore, the synthesis of the experience acquired by thousands of trained palates. There is no short cut to a knowledge of burgundy, but such symposia (I use the word in its original Greek sense) can save the learner from many detours, and even at times from culs-de-sac.

At tastings of burgundy, on the other hand, it is desirable to avoid conversation and concentrate on one's own findings. Also, at tastings of numerous bottles it is essential to avoid letting even a drop go down the gullet. Burgundies have a very pronounced taste, and if one is taking them in rapid succession even a small swallow of wine no. 1 will vitiate your judgement of wine no. 2, and so on through the tasting list.

At a tasting, after following the prescription of the host in the last paragraph but one, up to the point of sipping, one proceeds to 'chew' it in the mouth, to familiarize all the taste-buds with its quality, and then one must spit it out completely.

Wine usually tastes best from a glass, but the shape of the shallow silver Burgundian *tastevin*, besides revealing with peculiar accuracy the colour and clarity of the wine, does enable one to take a larger and more satisfactory mouthful for tasting than one would imbibe at a meal when actually drinking the wine.

I have never been able to decide, at a tasting of both, whether one should drink the whites first and the reds next, or vice versa. One would think, from the ordinary order of wine-service, that the whites should precede, but as one usually ends the whites with a fine Puligny- or Chassagne-Montrachet, the first little reds are then overwhelmed. I think the answer is that, unless one is a professional, one should stick to one colour only at a tasting.

But to revert, in conclusion, to drinking burgundy, not just to tasting it, a little trouble in the preparation and a little care in the service are certainly justified by the results. Apart from what one owes to one's guests, one has spent a fair amount even for a modest bottle. It is surely sensible to help it to show itself at its best.

Epilogue

I have played the candid friend to burgundy, stressing the difficulties of its climate, avowing the tricks that are played on it at home and cautioning the reader against the false labelling from which it suffers even abroad. I have painted the portrait with 'all these roughnesses, pimples, warts and everything as you see'.

A French apophthegm says: 'The more difficult the task, the more glorious the achievement.' It is a glorious thing to know burgundy. Not that it is really so difficult as all that. It is perfectly possible for any interested buyer, with a little knowledge and care, and reasonable expenditure, to get authentic versions of this capricious but fascinating wine. And when he does so, even if it is in quite modest bottles, the reward is great.

Burgundy is what the Germans call a *lebensjahende* wine, a wine that makes one say Yes to life. It has a tonic quality, as has long been recognized by old ladies in residential hotels, even if their restricted purses compel them to seek its restorative qualities in flagons of so-called burgundy from Australia. George Saintsbury in his *Notes on a Cellar-Book*, speaks of Richebourg in particular as a wine that will bring a man back from the shades, or indeed enable him to face any difficult adventure.

You may object that this can be said of many kinds of wine. What, it seems to me, is peculiar to burgundy is its quality of gusto, and as Max Beerbohm said, 'Gusto is an immense virtue. Gusto goes a huge long way.' As Max's character was not notably stamped with this quality, his tribute to it is the more convincing.

Burgundy is a big wine, but not a rough or overpowering one. It is what Horace called *Totus, teres atque rotundus* – entire, smooth and round. Nothing better promotes the sense of well-being than a well-selected burgundy. It increases the enjoyment of food, and facilitates digestion. Its drinking releases bonhomie. (Burgundy, I think, from an impudent young beaujolais to a mellow *cru* of the Côte de Nuits, evokes good humour; whereas the more ascetic claret is apt to induce a sardonic wit.) And though not cheap, it is still far less expensive than numerous less satisfying indulgences. I have paid out little money to better end than that which I have spent on sound burgundy.

As in no other field, the fine white burgundies share these qualities with the red. Le Montrachet provides an experience unique in the sphere of white table wine. Even the bouquet of an elegant Meursault will bring back youth in a sun-swept garden, or a book of verses underneath the bough. Better still, it will recall 'Thou beside me . . . Paradise enow!'

Various writers on burgundy, emulating the official classification of the Gironde, have essayed to set out a table of precedence of the great *crus* of the Côte d'Or, one even with a fanciful arrangement with Chambertin as the king, Romanée-Conti as the queen, and a suite of courtiers of different ranks of the peerage from dukes down. Now I am sure that all these tabulators are greater authorities than I, but I do know a good burgundy when I drink one, so I shall dare to list my personal evaluation of these vineyards, if only to provoke controversy. I started my tabulation with five categories, to correspond with the official listing of the Médoc; but I found this was leading me into nuances too subtle, and I reduced the divisions to three.

I take these wines by the average of the half century that I have known, and avoid invidiousness within ranks by using alphabetic order. My list is without prejudice in the legal sense of the phrase, but doubtless with some prejudice as the word is normally used. I apologize to the proprietors of numerous fine *crus* that I omit, either because I do not know them well or have not had the fortune to meet them at their best – and, for that matter, to prevent my selection from getting too diffuse. Many vineyards relegated to the excluded D category nevertheless make fine wines, taking precedence over all table wines except those of Bordeaux, the Rhine and the Moselle. The key to the *commune* initials (in brackets) is given at the end of the tabulation, and the vineyards marked with an asterisk★ belong to the Hospices de Beaune.

Here then is my version of the red hierarchy:

A

Chambertin (GC)   Clos de Bèze (GC)   Romanée-Conti (VR)

B

Bonnes Mares (MSD & CM)	Latricières-Chambertin (GC)
Chapelle-Chambertin (GC)	Mazis-Chambertin (GC)
Charmes-Chambertin (GC)	Musigny (CM)
Clos des Lambrays (MSD)	Dr Peste★ (AC)
Clos de Tart (MSD)	Richebourg (VR)
Clos de Vougeot (parts) (VO)	Nicolas Rolin★ (B)
Le Corton (AC)	La Romanée (VR)
Corton Clos du Roi (AC)	Romanée-St-Vivant (VR)
Dames Hospitalières★ (B)	Ruchottes-Chambertin (GC)
Echézeaux (VR)	Les Saint-Georges (NSG)
Grands Echézeaux (VR)	Guigone de Salins★ (B)
Griotte-Chambertin (GC)	La Tâche (VR)

C

Amoureuses (CM)	Boudriottes (CHM)
Beaux-Monts (VR)	Bressandes (AC)
Blondeau★ (V)	Bressandes (B)
Boudots (NSG)	Brunet★ (B)

Caillerets (V)
Cailles (NSG)
Champans (V)
Clos de la Commaraine (PO)
Clos des Forêts (PR)
Clos de la Maréchale (PR)
Clos des Mouches (B)
Clos de la Perrière (F)
Clos de la Roche (MSD)
Clos St-Denis (MSD)
Clos St-Jacques (GC)
Clos St-Jean (CHM)
Corvées (PR)
Didiers (PR)
Charlotte Dumay* (AC)
Epenots (PO)
Fèves (B)

Grande-Rue (VR)
Grèves (B)
Malconsorts (VR)
Marconnets (B)
Jehan de Massol* (V)
Murgers (NSG)
Général Muteau* (V)
Porets (NSG)
Pruliers (NSG)
Renardes (AC)
Rugiens (PO)
Santenots (M & V)
Suchots (VR)
Vaucrains (NSG)
Aux Vergelesses (SB)
Ile des Vergelesses (PV)
Veroilles (GC)

Now for a shot at the hierarchy of the whites. Fortunately there is no argument about the first category:

A

Le Montrachet (PM & CHM)

B

Bâtard-Montrachet
  (PM & CHM)
Bienvenues-Bâtard-
  Montrachet (PM)
Charmes (best vineyards) (M)
Chevalier-Montrachet (PM)

Corton-Charlemagne (AC)
Genevrières (M)
Loppin* (M)
Musigny blanc (CM)
Perrières (M)
François de Salins* (AC)

C

___

Blagny (M & PM)	Goutte d'Or (M)
Cailleret (PM)	Jehan Humblot* (M)
Charmes (other vineyards) (M)	
Clos des Mouches (B)	Morgeot (CHM)
Clos blanc de Vougeot (VO)	Pucelles (PM)
Combettes (PM)	Ruchottes (CHM)

* Means a vineyard of the Hospices de Beaune.

Key to commune initials:

AC Aloxe-Corton; B Beaune; CM Chambolle-Musigny; CHM Chassagne-Montrachet; F Fixin; GC Gevrey-Chambertin; M Meursault; MSD Morey-St-Denis; NSG Nuits-St-Georges; PM Puligny-Montrachet; PO Pommard; PR Premeaux; PV Pernand-Vergelesses; SB Savigny-les-Beaune; V Volnay; VO Vougeot; VR Vosne-Romanée.

Now if one were to bring chablis into consideration I think all the *grands crus* could fall into my B class of the whites, and certainly Grenouilles and Vaudésir would. The other *grands crus*, Blanchots, Bougros, Les Clos, Preuses, and Valmur would undeniably make the C grade, and perhaps also Fourchaume, Lys, Monts-de-Milieu and Montée de Tonnerre of the 1st *crus*.

There are a few proprietary wines that come up to the levels of the 1st *cru* single vineyards, among which I particularly respect Louis Latour's Corton-Grancey for a red and de Moucheron's Château de Meursault for a white.

Now as soon as one has committed oneself to such dispositions one begins to see anomalies in them. One remembers Richebourgs and Musignys, for example, that it seems absurd to put in any second class. One recalls bottles of Renardes that have been better than the neighbouring Clos du Roi. Fortunately this is not like an Oxford class list of a single year, in which a First will advantage a man's whole life, in comparison with the good Second that came so near to it; and in which any Second will be worth so much more to the recipient than the best Third. The list is just an unofficial and personal expression of opinion. And I have been speaking of averages. Generally Romanée-Conti and the Chambertins are better than Richebourg and Musigny, generally Clos du Roi is better than Renardes. But it is often a photo-finish.

Now as to the red *commune* wines of the Côte d'Or, I have already recorded my belief that Gevrey-Chambertin usually comes first. It is followed very closely, I think, by Vosne-Romanée and quite closely by Chambolle-Musigny. Then I should slip in Aloxe-Corton from the Côte de Beaune, though Morey-St-Denis, when you can get it, is excellent. Nuits-St-Georges, Beaune, Pommard and even Volnay depend so much on their authenticity; anyway I think I should prefer a Chassagne-Montrachet in a blind purchase. But in France I should put Nuits first, Volnay second and Beaune and Pommard level. Fixin, non-*clos* wines of Vougeot and Flagey-Echézeaux I do not rank very high; but the wines of some minor *communes* of the Côte de Beaune, Pernand-Vergelesses, Savigny and Auxey-Duresses are apt to surprise one by their merit, probably just because they are authentic.

Of the white *commune* wines my experience is that Meursault usually comes top. I believe that the Pulignys are better than the Chassagnes, but for personal reasons I prefer the latter. And hereabouts comes competition from the Mâconnais, in the form of the Pouilly-Fuissés, which can be very good indeed – or rather ordinary.

While trying to settle these classifications in my mind I was moved to ponder how one analyses the differentiation of good, fine and great wines. It seems to me that this can best be conveyed by an analogy from music – though I have already admitted that it is dangerous to transfer the perceptions of one sense to another. However, my comparison seems illuminating, to me at any rate. Well then, all wine strikes a note on the palate; good wine, with its greater subtlety, strikes a chord. Is it too fanciful to go further and say that fine wine plays a scale, but it is a diatonic scale, while great wine plays a chromatic one? And none of these scales of taste is more richly harmonic than those struck by the great burgundies.

I have purposely tried to write this book in a quiet and detached tone. Some of the French writing in particular, about wine, is apt to be too highly coloured. Ecstasies on this subject can have an effect on the reader opposite to that intended. But finally enthusiasm will break through. However, in conclusion, I shall let famous men speak for me rather than provide my own peroration.

Rabelais, though a Tourangeot, made Panurge rhapsodize about Beaune. Huysmans, quoted by Morton Shand, has a character proclaim that the great Côte de Nuits *cuvées* made abbatial processions file before his imagination, princely festivals, opulence of robes sewn with gold and afire with light. Meredith has one who exclaims that the second glass of an old Romanée or Musigny will be 'a High Priest for the uncommon nuptials between the body and soul of men'. Erasmus, defending himself against a charge of drinking Pommard on a fast-day, said more prosaically that his heart was Catholic, but for such wine his stomach was Protestant. An otherwise unknown bishop of Lyon, accused of using expensive *têtes de cuvée* from the Côte d'Or for sacramental wine, replied that he could not be seen making a wry face when he confronted his master. Another prelate, Bossuet (himself from Chenove, a famous field in his time), described burgundy as the *source de force et de joie*. Finally Brillat-Savarin, father and foremost of gastronomic writers, called it 'the most beautiful eulogy of God'.

On that note, I think, I can leave it.

Appendix A: Vintage Chart

The Wine & Food Society's Vintage Chart, originated by André Simon and much copied since, rates each year from zero for 'no good' to 7 for best. This has suggested the format for my own chart below. It is constructed from my personal recollection and notes, and may be a point or so out, one way or the other, in any given year, through the good or bad luck of my experience. I have, however, checked it against the tabulations of others, and find no substantial disagreements. This chart, like all such, must be taken with the well-known qualification that even in a 2 year some good bottles can be found, even in a 7 year there are flabby or thin wines. ('There are no good vintages, there are only good bottles,' said Albert Thibaudet, a great Burgundian; which perhaps is over-stated, but still provides a salutary caution.)

My recollection and notes for chablis do not go as far back as those for the Côte d'Or; nor do they do so for the Mâconnais and Beaujolais except for 1945, which I remember as a brilliant year there also. In any event, few possess, or could still buy, bottles of these distant vintages. Indeed, the first ten years of the table are probably only of historic interest.

The judgements on the last two or three years must be accepted with reserve; wines do not always develop as they promise, and sometimes they age better than had been expected.

For those lucky enough to have any of these 1940 and 1950 decades of red burgundy, all but the very greatest *crus* should be used up quickly, except that 1957 should last till about 1974. Of the 1960 vintage and after, '61 and '64 promise to last for some more years yet, say till 1975. These two years show staying power in the whites also, and they should retain their quality for ten or twelve years from their birth.

My own knowledge of the vintages of the Côte d'Or goes back to the great 1911s and '23s, drunk after the First War, probably with-

	Côte d'Or red	white	Chablis	Beaujolais/Mâconnais red	white	
1945	7	6		7	6	1945
1946	4	5				1946
1947	7	7				1947
1948	5	5				1948
1949	6	6	7	6	5	1949
1950	4	5	5	4	5	1950
1951	2	2	2	2	2	1951
1952	6	6	5	5	6	1952
1953	6	5	6	7	5	1953
1954	4	3	2	3	3	1954
1955	5	6	5	6	6	1955
1956	2	3	★	2	2	1956
1957	5	5	★	5	5	1957
1958	3	4	4	4	4	1958
1959	6	7	7	5	7	1959
1960	4	3	3	3	3	1960
1961	6	7	7	7	6	1961
1962	5	5	5	5	5	1962
1963	3	3	4	3	3	1963
1964	6	6	6	6	6	1964
1965	2	3	2	2	2	1965
1966	6	5	5	6	5	1966
1967	5	5	5	4	5	1967
1968	2	3	3	3	3	1968
1969	7	7	6	6	6	1969
1970	5	6	6	5	6	1970
1971	6	6	6	6	6	1971
1972	?5	?5	?5	?2	?5	1972

★ A tiny harvest: I have not drunk any.

out sufficient appreciation of them, and the excellent '21s and '26s. 1929 was a superb year, but followed by three failures. I had got in some '33s and '34s before the Second World War came; they matured quickly and were very helpful during the meagre years after the fall of France. After the war I tasted some '37s, which were more than acceptable; then the next vintage I knew was '45, splendid, but tantalizingly slow to develop when our cellars had such need of reinforcement. It was probably the experience of that year that turned the thoughts of so many proprietors and shippers to the *méthode nouvelle*.

For the historic record, André Simon, in his *Vintagewise*, speaks of 1865 and '75 as amazing vintages that lasted into the 1930s. Saintsbury praises 1869, '77 and '86 wines as 'delightful' – a rather feeble word. The last great pre-phylloxera year was 1889. There were no really good burgundies in the 1890s. Simon says that 1906 was the first great vintage of the twentieth century.

Camille Rodier takes matters back even further. Apparently conditions were not easy in Burgundy at the beginning of the great epoch of wine. In the forty-four vintages from 1787 to 1830, he states, only sixteen yielded good quantities and only seven were of good quality also. The famous 'year of the comet', 1811, was said by old authorities to have been the most magnificent of all.

My impression, on studying the old records, is that we have fewer complete failures now, with the improved methods of viticulture (though 1963, 1965 and 1968 came uncomfortably close together), and more average to good years; but none with the prestigious staying power of some nineteenth-century burgundies.

Appendix B: The *Grands* and 1st *Crus* of the Côte d'Or

The list follows the official *AC* classification. However, the names of certain vineyards are preceded by an asterisk, to denote that they have been accepted by certain authorities as superior 1st growths, or as better-known in export markets. The figures in brackets after each name represent the vineyards' acreages. The sizes of a few are omitted, since it has been impossible to ascertain these, for various reasons: either because of the amiable local practice of giving the same vineyard different names in different lists, or because of the failure to separate the classified part of a vineyard from the non-classified, or finally because in some cases the acreage is simply passed over in the official publications. In any event the dimensions are approximate, as no attempt has been made to translate the odd *ares* and *centiares* of land into British measurements. I have taken the area to the nearest *hectare*. The spelling of the vineyard names is very inconsistent, even in Burgundian publications.

1. *Côte de Nuits*

FIXIN

1st *crus*

Arvelets ($7\frac{1}{2}$)   Hervelets ($7\frac{1}{2}$)
Cheusots ($2\frac{1}{2}$)   Meix-Bas ($7\frac{1}{2}$)
*Clos du Chapître (10)   *Perrière (10)

BROCHON

Brochon has neither *grands* nor 1st *crus*.

EVREY-CHAMBERTIN

Grands crus:

Chambertin (32½)
Chambertin Clos de Bèze (37½)
Chapelle-Chambertin (17½)
Charmes- (or Mazoyères-)
   Chambertin (35)

Griotte-Chambertin (5)
Latricières-Chambertin (15)
Mazis-Chambertin (20)
Ruchottes-Chambertin (7½)

1st *crus:*

Bel Air
Cazetiers (20)
Champeaux (15)
Champonnets (7½)
Champitonnois (also called
   Petite Chapelle) (17½)
Cherbaudes (5)
Closeau
Clos du Chapître
*Clos St-Jacques (also called
   Village St-Jacques) (17½)
Clos Prieur (5)
Combe-aux-Moines (5)

Combottes(12½)
Corbeaux (7½)
Craipillot (5)
Ergots
Estournelles (2½)
Fonteny (9)
Gémeaux (5)
Goulots
Issarts
Lavaut (22½)
Perrière (5)
Poissenot
*Veroilles (15)

MOREY ST-DENIS

Grands crus:

Bonnes Mares (a small part) (2½)
Clos de la Roche (10)

Clos St-Denis (5)
Clos de Tart (17½)

1st *crus:*

Bouchots
Calouères (2½)
Chabiots (5)
Chaffots (2½)
Charmes (2½)
Charrières (5)

Chénevery (7½)
Clos Baulet (5)
Clos Bussière (7½)
*Clos des Lambrays (also
   known as Larrets) (20)
Clos des Ormes (10)

Clos Sorbés (5)
Côte Rôtie (5)
Façonnières (2½)
Fremières (5)
Froichots (5)
Genevrières (7½)
Gruenchers (7½)
Maison Brûlée (2½)

Mauchamps (5)
Meix-Rentiers (2½)
Millandes (10)
Monts-Luisants (white) (7½)
Riotte (5)
Ruchots (5)
Sorbés (7½)

CHAMBOLLE-MUSIGNY

Grands crus:

Bonnes Mares (also in Morey-St-Denis) (33½)
Clos de Tart (usually assigned to Morey-St-Denis, but the greater part is in Chambolle-Musigny) (17½)

Musigny (25, of which a little white)

1st crus:

*Amoureuses (12½)
Baudes (7½)
Beaux Bruns (5)
Borniques (2½)
*Charmes (12½)
Chatelots (5)
Combottes (5)
Aux Combottes (5)
Cras (10)
Derrière la Grange (10)

Fousselottes (10)
Fuées (15)
Groseilles (2½)
Gruenchers (5)
Hauts Doix (2½)
Lavrottes (2½)
Noirots (5)
Plantes (5)
Sentiers (10)

VOUGEOT

Grand cru:

Clos de Vougeot (125 acres)

1st *crus* red:

Cras (10)

Clos de la Perrière
Petits Vougeots (12½)

1st *cru* white:

Vigne Blanche or Clos Blanc
  de Vougeot (4½)

FLAGEY-ECHÉZEAUX

Flagey-Echézeaux has neither *grands* nor 1st *crus*, since Echézeaux, Grands Echézeaux and Beaux Monts are included in Vosne-Romanée.

VOSNE-ROMANÉE

Grands crus:

Echézeaux (75)
Grands Echézeaux (22½)
Richebourg (20)
La Romanée (5½)

Romanée-Conti (4½)
Romanée-St-Vivant (23)
La Tâche (15)

1st *crus:*

*Beaux-Monts (12½)
Brûlées (10)
Chaumes (17½)
Clos des Réas (5)
*Gaudichots (now in La
  Tâche) (15)

*Grande-Rue (2½)
*Malconsorts (9)
Petits Monts (7½)
Reignots (4½)
*Suchots (33½)

NUITS-ST-GEORGES AND PREMEAUX

(The 1st *crus* of Premeaux are entitled to use the *appellation* Nuits-St-Georges, and usually do so, so they are included, marked (P), in this list.)

1st *crus:*

Aux Argillats (20)
Les Argillats (25)
★Boudots (15)
Bousselots (15)
★Cailles (10)
Chaboeufs (7½)
Chaignots (13)
Chaîne-Carteau (6)
Champs Perdix (5)
Clos des Argillières (P) (12½)
Clos Arlots (P) (20)
Clos des Corvées (P) (19)
Clos des Forêts (P) (12½)
Clos des Grandes Vignes (P) (5)
★Clos de la Maréchale (P) (25)
Clos St-Marc (P) (7½)
Corvées-Paget (P) (5)
Cras (7½)
Crots (15)
Damodes (33½)
Didiers (P) (7½)

Hauts Pruliers (11½)
Murgers (12½)
Aux Perdrix (P) (7½)
Perrière (7½)
Perrière-Noblet (5)
★Porets (17½)
Poulettes (5)
Sur Premeaux
Procès (5)
★Pruliers (17½)
Richemone (5½)
Roncières (5)
Rousselots (10)
Rue de Chaux (7½)
★Les Saint-Georges (17½)
Sur Nuits
Thorey (15½)
Vallerots (24)
★Vaucrains (15)
Vignes Rondes (8)

PRISSEY, COMBLANCHIEN and CORGOLOIN

Prissey, Comblanchien and Corgoloin have neither *grands* nor 1st *crus.*

2. *Côte de Beaune*

LADOIX-SERRIGNY

1st *crus:* (which may also be sold under the *appellation* Aloxe-Corton)

Basses Mourettes (2½)
Coutière (3½)
Grandes Lolières (7½)

Maréchaude (4½)
Petites Lolières (3)
Toppe au Vert (5)

ALOXE-CORTON

Grands crus:

Charlemagne (white – but no
wine under this *appellation* has
been marketed for some time)

Corton (33)
Corton-Charlemagne
(white) (40)

1st *crus:*

Chaillots (8)
Chaumes (2½)
*Clos du Roi (25)
Fournières (15)
Guérets (5)
*Languettes (21½)
Maréchaudes (3)

Meix (5)
en Pauland (6)
*Pougets (25)
*Renardes (37½)
Valozières (16)
Vercots (10)

PERNAND-VERGELESSES

1st *crus:* (which may also be sold under the *appellation* Aloxe-Corton)

Basses Vergelesses (also in
Savigny-les-Beaune) (45)
Caradeux (50)
Creux de la Net (7½)

Fichots (27½)
*Ile des Vergelesses (also in
Savigny-les-Beaune) (28)

SAVIGNY-LES-BEAUNE

1st *crus:*

Basses Vergelesses (4½)
*Bataillère (also called Aux
Vergelesses) (42½)
Charnières (5)
Clous (38)
*Dominodes (also called
Jarrons) (22½)
Fourneaux
Grands Liards (25)
Gravains (16½)

Guettes (53½)
Hauts Jarrons (15)
Hauts Marconnets (23)
Lavières (45)
*Marconnets (23)
Narbantons (25)
Petits Godeau (19)
Petits Liards
Peuillets (53)
Redrescuts (2½)

Rouvrettes (14½)
Serpentières (33½)
Talmettes (7½)

*Aux Vergelesses (also in
  Pernand-Vergelesses) (42½)

CHOREY-LES-BEAUNE

Chorey-Les-Beaune has neither *grands* nor 1st *crus*.

BEAUNE

1st *crus*:

Aigrots (37)
Avaux (33½)
Bas des Teurons
Blanches Fleurs (23)
Boucherottes (22)
*Bressandes (44)
Cent Vignes (58)
Champs Piment
Chouacheux (12½)
*Clos des Mouches (red and
  white) (37½)
Clos de la Mousse (8)
Clos du Roi (34)
Coucherias (57)
Cras (12½)
Ecu (7½)
Epenottes (35)
*Fèves (10½)

en Genêt (12½)
*Grèves (79½)
sur les Grèves (10)
*Marconnets (16)
Mignotte (5)
Montée Rouge (41)
Montrevenots (20)
en l'Orne (5)
Perrières (8)
Pertuisots (14)
Reversées (13)
Seurey (3)
Sisies (21)
*Teurons (38)
Tiélandry (also known as
  Clos Landry) (4)
Toussaints (15)
Vignes Franches (25)

POMMARD

1st *crus*:

Argillières (8½)
Arvelets (20)
Bertins (8½)
Boucherottes (4½)

Chanlins Bas (17½)
Chanière (25)
Chaponnières (8)
Les Charmots (7)

Clos Blanc (11)
*Clos de la Commaraine (10)
Clos Micot (7)
Clos du Verger (6)
Combes Dessus (7)
Croix Noires (10½)
Derrière St-Jean (3)
*Epenots (25)
Fremiers (12½)

Garollières (8)
Petits Epenots (51)
*Pézerolles (15)
*Platière (14)
Poutures (11)
Refène (6)
*Rugiens-Bas (15)
*Rugiens-Haut (14)
Sausilles (9)

VOLNAY

1st *crus*:

Angles (8)
Aussy (7½)
Barre (also called Clos de la Barre) (3)
Brouillards (17)
*Caillerets (36)
*Caillerets Dessus
Carelle Dessous (5)
Carelle sous la Chapelle (9½)
*Champans (28)
Chanlin (10)
Chevret (15)
Clos des Chênes (41)
Clos des Ducs (6)
Durets

Fremiets (15)
Lurets (20)
Mitans (10)
Ormeau (11)
Petures
Pitures Dessus (9)
Pointe d'Angles (3)
Pousse d'Or (5)
Robardelle (12)
Ronceret (5)
*Santenots (also in Meursault) (20)
Taille-Pieds (22)
Verseuil (18)
Village de Volnay (33½)

MONTHÉLIE

1st *crus*:

Cas Rougeot (3½)
Champs Fulliot (20)
Château Gaillard (5)
Clos Gauthey (8)
Duresses (also in Auxey-Duresses) (19)

Lavelle (9)
Meix-Bataille (6½)
Riottes (4)
Taupine (4)
Vignes Rondes (7)

AUXEY-DURESSES

1st *crus:*

Bas des Duresses (6½)
Bretterins (also known as La
    Chapelle)
Climat or Clos du Val (23)
Duresses (also in Monthélie) (19)

Ecusseaux (16)
Grands Champs (11)
Reugne (8)
Reugne (also called
    La Chapelle)

MEURSAULT

(Note: the comparatively rare red 1st *crus* are usually labelled as
Volnays.)

1st *crus:*

Bouchères (10½)
Caillerets (13)
★Charmes Dessous (31)
★Charmes Dessus (37½)
Cras (sometimes called Gras)
    (11)
★Genevrières Dessous and
    Genevrières Dessus
    (together 42½)
★Goutte d'Or (13)

Jennelotte (13)
★Perrières Dessous and ★Perrières
    Dessus (together 42½)
Petures (27½)
Pièce sous le Bois (28)
★Poruzots (8)
Poruzots Dessus (16½)
★Santenots Blancs (7½)
Santenots du Milieu (20)
Sous le Dos d'Ane (7½)

PULIGNY-MONTRACHET

Grands crus:

Bâtard-Montrachet (also in
    Chassagne-Montrachet) (25)
Chevalier-Montrachet (15½)

Bienvenues-Bâtard-Montrachet (6)
Montrachet (also in Chassagne-
    Montrachet) (10)

1st *crus:*

★Caillerets (12½)
Chalumeaux (17½)
Champ Canet (10½)

Clavoillons (13½)
★Combettes (16½)
Folatières (8)

Garenne
*Hameau de Blagny (11)
*Pucelles (16½)

Referts (34)
Sous le Puits (9½)

CHASSAGNE-MONTRACHET

Grands crus: (all white)

Bâtard-Montrachet (also in
  Puligny-Montrachet) (30)
Criots-Bâtard-Montrachet (4)

Montrachet (also in
  Puligny-Montrachet) (9)

1st *crus:* (all both red and white, except that En Cailleret produces red
        only and Cailleret, also known as Chassagne, produces white
        only)

Abbaye de Morgeot
*Boudriotte (45)
Brussolles (45)
*Cailleret (also known as
  Chassagne) and En Cailleret
  (together 15)
Champs Gain (71)
Chenevottes (28)

*Clos St-Jean (36)
*Grands Ruchottes (7½)
Macherelles (10)
Maltroie (23)
*Morgeot (9¾)
Romanée
Vergers (23)

ST-AUBIN

1st *crus:*

Champlot (20)
Chatenière (25)
Combes (37½)
Frionnes

Murgers des Dents de Chien (7½)
Remilly (5)
Sur Gamay (35)
Sur le Sentier du Clou

SANTENAY

1st *crus:* (red and white)

Beauregard (82)
Beaurepaire (42½)
Clos des Tavannes (66)
Comme (80)

*Gravières (72½)
Maladière (33)
Passe Temps (31)

CHEILLY-LES-MARANGES

1st *crus:* (red and white)
Boutières, Maranges and Plantes de Maranges (together 108)

DEZIZE-LES-MARANGES

1st *cru:* (red and white)
Maranges (150)

SAMPIGNY-LES-MARANGES

1st *crus:* (red and white)
Clos des Rois (36)   Maranges (35)

Appendix C. The Principal Vineyards of the Hospices de Beaune

Vineyard	Commune
RED	
Clos des Avaux	Beaune (Avaux)
Hugues & Louis Bétault	Beaune (Grèves & Aigrots)
Billardet	Pommard (Epenots & Noirons)
Boillot	Auxey-Duresses (Duresses)
Blondeau	Volnay (Champans & Taille-Pieds)
Brunet	Beaune (Bressandes & Mignotte)
Dames de la Charité	Pommard (Epenots & Rugiens)
Dames Hospitalières	Beaune (Bressandes & Mignotte)
Maurice Drouhin	Beaune (Avaux, Boucherottes, Champimonts & Grèves)
Charlotte Dumay	Aloxe-Corton (Renardes & Bressandes)
Estienne	Beaune (Perrières & Bressandes)
Fouquerand	Savigny-les-Beaune (Vergelesses & Gravains)
Forneret	Savigny-les-Beaune (Vergelesses & Gravains)
Gauvin	Volnay (Santenots)
Arthur Girard	Savigny-les-Beaune (Marconnets)
Rameau Lamarosse	Vergelesses (Basses Vergelesses)
Jacques Lebelin	Monthélie (Duresses)
Jehan de Massol	Volnay (Santenots)
Général Muteau	Volnay (Village & Carelle)
Docteur Peste	Aloxe-Corton (Bressandes & Clos du Roi)
Nicolas Rolin	Beaune (Cent-Vignes & Grèves)
Rousseau-Deslandes	Beaune (Cent-Vignes & Montrevenots)

Vineyard	Commune

RED

Guigone de Salins	Beaune (Bressandes & Champimonts)
Pierre Virely	Beaune (Montée Rouge)

Vineyard	Commune

WHITE

de Bahèzre de Lanlay	Meursault (Charmes)
Baudot	Meursault (Genevrières)
Philippe le Bon	Meursault (Genevrières)
Goureau	Meursault (Poruzots)
Albert Grivault	Meursault (Charmes)
Jehan Humblot	Meursault (Poruzots)
Loppin	Meursault (Criots)
François de Salins	Aloxe-Corton (Charlemagne)

The biggest output among the reds comes from Charlotte Dumay (some 700 cases on an average), followed by Guigone de Salins, Dames Hospitalières and Clos des Avaux. The smallest comes from Pierre Virely and Gauvin (some 120 cases each). The white output is much smaller. All of these white vineyards are about the same size, averaging some 375 cases, except de Bahèzre de Lanlay, which averages about 140 only.

Appendix D: Classifications of Chablis, the Chalonnais, Mâconnais and Beaujolais

I. CHABLIS

Grands crus: Blanchots, Bougros, Clos, Grenouilles, Preuses, Valmur, Vaudésir. (Note: there is a proprietary wine called La Moutonne that has been accepted as a *grand cru*.)

1st crus: Beugnons, Boroy (or Beaurroy), Butteaux (also called Vaugerlans), Châpelots, Châtains, Côte de Fontenay, Côte de Léchet, Forêts, Fourchaume, Lys, Mélinots, Monts de Milieu, Montée-de-Tonnerre, Montmains, Pied d'Aloup, Roncières, Séché (also called Epinottes), Troême, Vaillons, Vaucoupin, Vaugiraud, Vaulorent, Vaupulent, Vosgros

Other wines of this area are sold, according to quality, as (1) Chablis, (2) Petit Chablis.

II. THE CHALONNAIS

Mercurey (95% red): This *appellation* can be used either with the name of its vineyards – Clos des Montaigus, Clos des Fourneaux, Clos Marcilly, Clos du Roi, Clos Voyen, etc. – see page 104 – or as Mercurey 1st *cru*.

Givry (nearly all red)

Rully (20% red, 80% white): This *appellation* can be used either with the name of its vineyard – Bressandes, Champ-Clou, Chapître, Cloux, Ecloseaux, Fosse, Grésigny, Margotey, Marisson, Meix-Caillet, Mont-Palais, Moulesne, Pierres, Pillot, Préau, Raboursay, Raclot, Renardes, Vauvry – or as Rully 1st *cru*.

Montagny (all white)

Other wines of this area are sold, according to quality, as (1) *bourgogne* or (2) *bourgogne grand ordinaire*.

III. THE MÁCONNAIS

Pouilly-Fuissé
Pouilly-Vinzelles
Pouilly-Loché   } (white only)
St-Véran

Other wines of this area are sold, according to quality, as (1) Mâcon Supérieur, Mâcon followed by the name of the *commune* of origin, or (for whites) as Mâcon Villages, or (2) as Mâcon.

IV. THE BEAUJOLAIS.

Brouilly	Juliénas
Chénas	Morgon
Chiroubles	Moulin-à-Vent
Côte de Brouilly	St-Amour
Fleurie	

Other wines of this area are sold, according to quality, as (1) Beaujolais Villages or Beaujolais followed by the name of any of the following areas of origin – Arbuissonas, Beaujeu, Blancé, Cercié, Chânes, Chapelle-de-Guinchay, Cherentay, Chénas, Chiroubles, Denicé, Durette, Emeringes, Fleurie, Juliénas, Jullié, Lancié, Lantigné, Leynes, Montmelas, Odenas, Perréon, Pruzilly, Quincié, Regnié, Rivolet, Romanèche, St-Amour-Bellevue, St-Etienne-des-Ouillères, St-Etienne-la-Varenne, Ste-Julié, St-Lager, St-Symphorien-d'Ancelles, St-Vérand, Salles, Vaux, Villié-Morgon; (2) Beaujolais Supérieur; (3) Beaujolais.

Appendix E: Minimum Alcoholic Strengths of Various Burgundies

I. CÔTE D'OR

	red	white
	degrees	

	red degrees	white degrees
Côte de Nuits; *grands crus*	11·5	12*
1st *crus*	11	11·5
commune wines	10·5	11
Vins fins de la Côte de Nuits, or Côte de Nuits Villages	10·5	11
Côte de Beaune; Montrachet, Chevalier-Montrachet, Corton & Corton-Charlemagne		12
Other *grands crus*	11·5	11·5
1st *crus*	11	11·5
commune wines	10·5	11
Côte de Beaune	10·5	11
Côte de Beaune Villages	10·5	

II. CHABLIS

Grands crus		11
1st *crus*		10·5
Chablis		10
Petit Chablis		9

III. CHALONNAIS

	red	white
Mercurey, Montagny and Rully, 1st growths	11	11·5
Givry and others	10·5	11

IV. MÂCONNAIS

	red	white
Pouilly-Fuissé, -Loché and -Vinzelles		12
Other named *crus*		11
Mâcon Supérieur and named *communes*	10	11
Mâcon Villages		11
Mâcon	9	10

V. BEAUJOLAIS

9 named *crus* coupled with name of vineyard	11†	
Côte de Brouilly	10·5	
Other 8 named *crus*	10	
Beaujolais Villages	10	10·5
Beaujolais Supérieur	10	10·5
Beaujolais	9	9·5

VI. MISCELLANEOUS

Bourgogne	10	10·5
Bourgogne grand ordinaire or *ordinaire*	9	9·5
Passe-tout-grains	9·5	
Bourgogne rosé	10	
Bourgogne aligoté		9·5
Sparkling burgundy	9	9·5
Marc de Bourgogne		40

* This is the rare Musigny *blanc*.

† i.e. Brouilly, Chénas, Chiroubles, Côte de Brouilly, Fleurie, Juliénas, Morgon, Moulin-à-vent, St-Amour, if a vineyard name is added.

Appendix F: Maximum *AC* Yields per Acre

(Note: these yields may be increased by special permission – and often are so – in prolific years; but the comparative figures of the regular maxima indicate the comparative qualities. The figures given represent the output at vinification, after which there is inevitably loss through wastage, so the number of bottles actually made is lower than the figures given.)

	No. of bottles per acre
1. *Grands crus* of the Côte d'Or	1609
2. Chablis *grands crus*, 1st *crus* and *commune* wines of the Côte d'Or, Vins fins de la Côte de Nuits, Côte de Beaune, Côte de Beaune Villages, Mercurey	1877
3. Chablis 1st *crus*, Chablis, Petit Chablis, Givry, Rully, Montagny, Beaujolais 1st *crus*	2170
4. Pouilly-Fuissé, -Loché and -Vinzelles, Mâcon *supérieur*, Beaujolais Villages, Beaujolais *supérieur*, *Bourgogne, Bourgogne grand ordinaire* or *ordinaire, Aligoté*	2414
5. *Passe-tout-grains*	2435
6. Mâcon, Beaujolais	2712

Appendix G: Some Burgundy Shippers

There are said to be over 250 shippers of burgundy, which I can well believe from the number of name-plates and advertisements seen during my visits to their country. The following list consists only of those known, or known of, by me. Undoubtedly it omits good names, but no one in the trade, let alone an amateur, can be familiar with all the houses. When my experience with a given shipper relates to particular wines I have noted this in brackets, but this does not imply that the house in question may not be equally competent for other burgundies. I have prefaced a few names with asterisks, to denote those whose shipments or bottlings I have recently enjoyed to my personal satisfaction.

Marcel Baron
Bouchard Aîné
*Bouchard Père & Fils
Louis Bouillot
  (sparkling burgundy)
*J. Calvet & Cie
Cartron & Cie (cassis, marc)
*Chanson Père & Fils
F. Chauvenet
Lupé Cholet & Cie
Coron Père & Fils
Paul Court
Jacques Dépagneux (beaujolais)
*Joseph Drouhin & Cie
*M. Doudet-Naudin
Georges Duboeuf (beaujolais)
*J. Faiveley
Georges Favrot (beaujolais)
Geisweiler & Fils
Grivelet Père & Fils

Jaboulet-Verchère
*Louis Jadot
*Louis Latour & Cie
Leroy
Comte B. de Lescure (beaujolais)
*Lebègue-Bichot & Cie
C. Marey Liger-Belair
de Marcilly Frères
Louis Michel (chablis)
*J. Mommesin
A. Morel (beaujolais)
J. Moreau (chablis)
René Morey (Meursault)
Morin Père & Fils (Clos
  Vougeot)
*de Moucheron & Cie
Pasquier-Desvignes & Cie
Patriarche Père & Fils
Piat Père & Fils (beaujolais)
Brac de la Perrière (beaujolais)

Pierre Picard
Pierre Ponnelle
Poulet Père & Fils
★A. Regnard & Fils (chablis)
Jules Regnier & Cie
J. H. Remy
Remoissenet Père & Fils
★J. B. Reynier Ltd
Ropiteau Frères (Meursault)
L. Rosenheim & Sons Ltd
Armand Rousseau
René Roy

Sichel & Cie
Sichel & Fils Frères
Comte de Sparre (Moulin-à-Vent)
Roland Thévenin (Puligny-Montrachet)
★J. Thorin & Cie (beaujolais)
Charles Vienot
★Marcel Vincent (Pouilly-Fuissé)
★Comte Georges de Voguë (Musigny)

Bibliography

I have read scores, if not hundreds, of books about wine, and none of them has failed to throw some light on burgundy, if only by comparison or contrast. The following list of books, read or re-read while I was compiling this volume, may be of help to those, if any, in whom it has induced a desire for further study of this subject.

A Book of Burgundy – Pictures and Talks on the Wine of Burgundy, Lund Humphries.

CARTER, YOUNGMAN, *Drinking Burgundy*, Hamish Hamilton, 1966.

DAVID, ELIZABETH, *French Provincial Cooking*, Penguin Books, 1970.

DION, *Histoire de la Vigne et du Vin de France*, Dion, Paris.

ENGEL, RENÉ, *Vade Mecum Oenologique*, Maurice Pouvot, Paris.

FORGEOT, PIERRE, *Guide de l'Amateur de Bourgogne*, Confrérie des Chevaliers du Tastevin, Nuits-St-Georges.

HYAMS, EDWARD, *Dionysus*, Thames & Hudson, 1965.

JACQUELIN, LOUIS, and POULAIN, RENÉ, *The Wines and Vineyards of France*, Paul Hamlyn, 1962.

JEFFS, JULIAN, *The Wines of Europe*, Faber and Faber, 1971.

JOHNSON, HUGH, *Wine*, Nelson, 1966.
The World Atlas of Wine, Mitchell Beazley, 1971.

LARMAT, L., *Atlas de la France Vinicole – les Vins de Bourgogne*, L. Larmat, Paris.

LICHINE, ALEXIS, *Wines of France*, Cassell, 1969.

POUPON, PIERRE, and FORGEOT, PIERRE, *The Wines of Burgundy* (English edition), Presses Universitaires de France, Paris.

RODIER, CAMILLE, *Le Vin de Bourgogne*, L. Damidot, Dijon.

SHAND, P. MORTON, *A Book of French Wines* (revised and edited by Cyril Ray), Penguin Books, 1964.

SIMON, ANDRÉ L., *The Commonsense of Wine*, The Wine & Food Society and Michael Joseph, 1966.

The Noble Grapes and the Great Wines of France, McGraw-Hill, London, 1957.

Vintagewise, Michael Joseph, 1945.

Wines of the World (edited and partly written by André L. Simon), McGraw-Hill, 1967.

VANDYKE PRICE, PAMELA, *France – a food and wine guide*, Tom Stacey, 1972.

YOUNGER, WILLIAM, *Gods, Men and Wine*, The Wine & Food Society and Michael Joseph, 1966.

Index

More about Penguins
and Pelicans

Penguinews, which appears every month, contains
details of all the new books issued by Penguins as
they are published. From time to time it is
supplemented by *Penguins in Print*, which is a
complete list of all available books published by
Penguins. (There are well over four thousand
of these.)

A specimen copy of *Penguinews* will be sent to
you free on request. For a year's issues (including
the complete lists) please send 30p if you live in
the United Kingdom, or 60p if you live elsewhere.
Just write to Dept EP, Penguin Books Ltd,
Harmondsworth, Middlesex, enclosing a cheque or
postal order, and your name will be added to the
mailing list.

Note: *Penguinews* and *Penguins in Print* are not
available in the U.S.A. or Canada

The Penguin Book of
Home Brewing and Wine-Making

W. H. T. Tayleur

Home brewing has been a tradition in this country ever since the Druids were recognized as masters of the craft. W. H. T. Tayleur, an expert in the field of beer and wine-making, here provides a comprehensive guide which will be invaluable both to the beginner and to the more experienced brewer. Here is all you need to know about beer and wine, liqueurs and cider, perry and mead: how to make them, how to bottle and store them and how to serve them.

Enthusiasts will welcome, in particular, the long section on the art of home wine-making; pre-packed kits and grapejuice concentrates are now widely available and Mr Tayleur gives full directions for their use, as well as many delightful recipes for sparkling wines and for wines made from grapes, fruit of all varieties, vegetables and flowers.

The materials, in short, are all around us: and, with the help of this handbook, there is nothing to stop the intelligent layman from becoming an intelligent wine-maker . . . or brewer.

The Wines of Bordeaux

Edmund Penning-Rowsell

Revised Edition

The Wines of Bordeaux ('written by an interested
amateur for others who care to look beyond the bottle
and the label') offers both the layman and expert the only
comprehensive critical work on Bordeaux wines yet
published.

In the opening chapters Edmund Penning-Rowsell
describes the wine districts of the Gironde, listing the
types of grapes and wines found there: he then goes on
to chart the rise of the vineyard estates and the activities
of the wine merchants. He deals with each district in
turn, from those of the Médoc to those of the sweet
white wines, not forgetting the less well-known ones.
Finally, he discusses the famous – and controversial –
1855 classification and Bordeaux vintages from the end of
the eighteenth century. Included in the appendices are the
opening prices on classed growth since 1830 and rainfall
statistics.

'A most accurate, encyclopedic and immensely valuable
work' — *The Times Literary Supplement*

'The comprehensiveness and intellectual integrity of
The Wines of Bordeaux will ensure it an honoured place
on the shelves of every wine lover' – *Daily Telegraph*

Not for sale in the U.S.A.